Mixed Ability Grouping:
A Philosophical Perspective

Introductory Studies in Philosophy of Education
Series Editors: PHILIP SNELDERS and COLIN WRINGE

Education and the Value of Knowledge by M. A. B. Degenhardt
Can We Teach Children To Be Good? by Roger Straughan
Means and Ends in Education by Brenda Cohen
Mixed Ability Grouping: A Philosophical Perspective by
    Charles Bailey and David Bridges

Mixed Ability Grouping: A Philosophical Perspective

CHARLES BAILEY and
DAVID BRIDGES
Homerton College, Cambridge

London
GEORGE ALLEN & UNWIN
Boston   Sydney

**George Allen & Unwin (Publishers) Ltd,
40 Museum Street, London WC1A 1LU, UK**

George Allen & Unwin (Publishers) Ltd,
Park Lane, Hemel Hempstead, Herts HP2 4TE, UK

Allen & Unwin, Inc.,
9 Winchester Terrace, Winchester, Mass. 01890, USA

George Allen & Unwin Australia Pty Ltd,
8 Napier Street, North Sydney, NSW 2060, Australia

First published in 1983.

British Library Cataloguing in Publication Data

Bailey, Charles
 Mixed ability grouping.
1. Nongraded schools.
I. Title   II. Bridges, David
371.2'52   LB1029.N6
ISBN 0-04-370134-5
ISBN 0-04-370135-3 Pbk

Library of Congress Cataloging in Publication Data

Bailey, Charles.
 Mixed ability grouping.
(Introductory studies in philosophy of education)
Bibliography: p.
Includes index.
1. Ability grouping in education.   I. Bridges, David.
II. Title.   III. Series.
LB3061.B34   1983   371.2'52   83-3846
ISBN 0-04-370134-5
ISBN 0-04-370135-3 (pbk.)

Set in 11 on 12 point Plantin by
Computape (Pickering) Ltd, North Yorkshire
and printed in Great Britain by
Billing and Sons Ltd, London and Worcester

Books that are available to students of philosophy of education may, in general, be divided into two types. There are collections of essays and articles making up a more or less random selection; and there are books which explore a single theme or argument in depth but, having been written to break new ground, are often unsuitable for general readers or those near the beginning of their course. The Introductory Studies in Philosophy of Education are intended to fill what is widely regarded as an important gap in this range.

The series aims to provide a collection of short, readable works which, besides being philosophically sound, will seem relevant and accessible to future and existing teachers without a previous knowledge of philosophy or of philosophy of education. In the planning of the series account has necessarily been taken of the tendency of present-day courses of teacher education to follow a more integrated and less discipline-based pattern than formerly. Account has also been taken of the fact that students on three- and four-year courses, as well as those on shorter postgraduate and in-service courses, quite understandably expect their theoretical studies to have a clear bearing on their practical concerns, and on their dealings with children. Each book, therefore, starts from a real and widely recognised problem in the educational field, and explores the main philosophical approaches which illuminate and clarify it, or suggests a coherent standpoint even when it does not claim to provide a solution. Attention is paid to the work of both mainstream philosophers and philosophers of education. For students who wish to pursue particular questions in depth, each book contains a bibliographical essay or a substantial list of suggestions for further reading. It is intended that a full range of the main topics recently discussed by philosophers of education should eventually be covered by the series.

Besides having considerable experience in the teaching of philosophy of education, the majority of authors writing in the series have already received some recognition in their particular fields. In addition, therefore, to reviewing and criticising existing work, each author has his or her own positive contribution to make to further discussion.

PHILIP SNELDERS
COLIN WRINGE

Contents

To our wives,
Joyce and Angela

Introduction

It's becoming fashionable to say that the argument is no longer about why we unstream but how. I find this a disturbing view, because so often in educational innovation the way you do it depends on your reasons. It's fine at the beginning with perhaps a handful of teachers swept on to action by their enthusiasm and energy; the trouble begins when innovation has to be sustained by extending the original ideas and involving more and more staff ... Now more than ever, with money and staff getting scarcer, innovation needs to succeed and to gain the staffroom support of more than a few zealots. It needs to be done for the right reasons and in the case of non-streaming I don't think they are all that obvious. (Holt, 1976, p. 55)

Six years after Maurice Holt's contribution to a special issue of *Forum* on mixed ability grouping, his reference to the increasing scarcity of money and staff has a sharper significance than perhaps even he would have anticipated. In that same time, however, the enthusiasm for unstreaming has faltered, the pedagogic consequences and practical difficulties associated with the innovation have been seen in clearer perspective and even the principles underlying mixed ability organisation have come under renewed critical scrutiny.

The time seems ripe, then, for a new treatment of the arguments underlying the practice of mixed ability grouping. In any case, we believe that, notwithstanding some admirable reports and research inquiries, the philosophical foundations of the case in favour of mixed ability grouping have never been adequately laid. Typically, arguments in favour of mixed ability grouping have included reference to some ill-defined 'social benefits' or to egalitarian principles which their proponents have made little attempt to define or to justify. Without a reasonably clearly worked out view of what they are pursuing and why, teachers, as Holt suggests, are poorly prepared to sustain innovation, to justify it to those who legitimately demand such justification, or even to appreciate the full practical implications of what they are doing.

This book is written primarily in the hope that it will help teachers and interested persons outside schools to develop their understanding of the rationale of mixed ability grouping. It is not our intention simply to provide such a rationale all neatly worked out for deployment in staffroom argument or public debate. The argument invites, and we hope it will receive, the kind of critical attention which may lead some readers to conclusions contrary to our own. Whether the reader ends up supporting or opposing mixed ability grouping, we hope at least that that position will be based on a more thorough understanding of the principles which underlie it.

The book has a second and complementary purpose which is linked to its appearance in this series of Introductory Studies in Philosophy of Education. We hope that it will serve to illustrate the kind of contribution which philosophy of education can make to the examination of a practical educational problem. In this sense it may usefully serve as an introduction to philosophy of education. With this in mind we have tried to avoid or explain any particularly technical terms and have not assumed any special familiarity with the philosophical literature.

But though the approach of the book is largely philosophical in character, we have tried to relate philosophical considerations closely to practical and empirical perspectives and to teachers' experience of mixed ability grouping. We think it is nonsense, for example, to give an account of what mixed ability grouping 'means' without reference to the variety of practice which is picked out by teachers' actual use of the term (Chapter 1). We think it is useful to show something of the connection between more strictly philosophical arguments about equality, fraternity, and so on, and what teachers actually offer by way of rationale for mixed ability grouping (Chapter 2). We think it is perverse to construct a case in terms of the intended outcomes of mixed ability grouping without regard to the actual outcomes of different forms of school organisation (Chapter 6).

We believe that this approach is an appropriate one within philosophy of education and, more important, a necessary one if educational practices are to be rationally grounded. If we can do something to advance this last cause we will risk the accusation of 'impure' philosophy!

1

'Mixed Ability' – What do We Mean?

In asking what we mean when we talk about 'mixed ability groups' or 'mixed ability teaching' we are not announcing an attempt at close conceptual analysis. The concepts are in any case not sufficiently stable or firmly established to lend themselves readily to such analysis. What we do want to begin to identify is something of the range of practice whose logic and rationale it is the purpose of this book to examine. In this we are trying to avoid prescriptive or stipulative definition. We prefer to offer a relatively naturalistic account based on the existing literature and on the talk of practising teachers – to many of whom we are grateful for discussions which have gone to inform what follows.

Mixed Ability Classes

One does not need to attend long to the literature or talk on this subject to discover both a variety of practice which goes on under the name of 'mixed ability', especially in secondary schools which have 'unstreamed' as a matter of policy, and a variety of practice which could well go under the name but usually does not, notably in small infant and junior schools which have never seriously contemplated any alternative.

At secondary level few schools, if any, are organised in such a way that all classes from 11 to 16 are made up of groups reflecting the full range of ability in the school. The mixed ability organisation is typically limited to the first, second, or third year, or restricted to particular subjects whose character is thought to lend itself to work in mixed ability groups or whose teachers are ideologically committed to this pattern of organisation. Given this variety of practice Her Majesty's Inspectorate sought to establish a set of minimal criteria by which to identify a comprehensive school which was significantly attached to mixed ability work. They proposed 'one in which, at least up to the end of the third year of the normal secondary course, the curriculum was taught wholly or mainly i.e. with not more than two subjects excluded in classes in which the span of ability ranged from significantly below to significantly above average' (Department of Education and Science, 1978, p. 9). The definition draws attention to the two variables already referred to – the number of year-groups and the range of subjects which are taught in mixed ability groups – but adds a third significant consideration – the range of ability encompassed in the groups.

There are, of course, a number of factors which go to ensure that some classes include a much wider range of ability than others. It may be helpful to give these a brief mention.

(a) *The Character of the Intake of a School*

It is the constant complaint of some 'comprehensive' schools that they are not in fact fully comprehensive because of either the character of their catchment area or the presence nearby of another school which manages to 'cream off' the most able pupils. Some former secondary modern schools have barely extended the ability range that they used to receive in the days of formal selection. Equally, some schools have little experience of having to cope in their day-to-day work with, for example, pupils with only a limited command of English. A small rural primary school may arrange to accommodate within its ordinary classroom routine a child or children whose handicaps or disabilities would elsewhere lead them to be assigned to a special unit or a special school. The simple fact is that not all schools have to cope with anything like the same range of abilities or disabilities (cf. Monks, 1968; ILEA Inspectorate, 1976).

(b) *The Age-Range Encompassed in One Class*

Secondary schools in Britain on the whole assume that their classes will contain pupils born within a twelve-month period. This naturally tends to limit the diversity of attainment that one might find in a group, as compared, for example, with the range of reading ability one might find in a family grouped primary school. Interestingly, of course, a decision to break away from the chronological grouping could be taken with a view to achieving greater homogeneity in the group, as in the United States grading system, or might have the effect of greater heterogeneity, as in the family grouping pattern.

(c) *The Use of Special Provision in the School*

Some secondary schools which have adopted a general pattern of mixed ability grouping nevertheless make special arrangements for remedial work with the less able, which effectively means that classes rarely include the full range of ability represented in the school. Indeed, some take this policy a stage further to the point that, as Gough and McGhee (1977, p. 43) argue:

> Where a school has a relatively small range of ability in its population and forms, a 'remedial' group and, as happens sometimes, an accelerated group – 'topping and tailing' – one is led to ask questions about how 'mixed' are the groups in the middle, and how different this is from streaming.

(d) *The Way in which Classes Are Formed*

If you do not deliberately construct your classes on the basis of some assessment of ability, how do you do it? Typically perhaps schools may take into account considerations like maintaining an approximately even distribution of boys and

3

girls, separating trouble-makers, enabling friends to stay together. Beyond this they commonly resort to some apparently arbitrary measure like simply dividing up an alphabetical list. Such procedures do not, however, necessarily produce groups each of which contains the full spread of ability represented in the cohort of pupils. Schools firmly bent on achieving such a spread may need to employ some of the old tools of assessment to the new end of ensuring not homogeneous but heterogeneous classes.

But even then there are problems. For just as a supposedly 'streamed' school can result in what are in effect mixed ability classes, if the criteria on the basis of which they are streamed do not apply across the board, so would-be 'mixed ability schools' may find that they have generated relatively homogeneous groups in some subjects in which the criteria on which pupils were mixed do not appear to operate to the same effect. Those in favour of homogeneous grouping resorted to setting as a means of fine tuning their group composition. We are not aware of any unstreamed schools that have taken their advocacy of mixed ability groups to this length. Why this is so may turn out to be revealing of some of the complex motives schools have for favouring mixed ability grouping.

(e) *The Way the Curriculum Is Organised*

Fairly or unfairly, some secondary school subjects enjoy a reputation for being more academically demanding than others. Some schools deliberately introduce options designed to be more intellectually accessible to students who are struggling with an apparently more demanding element of the curriculum – for instance, a largely descriptive 'French studies' as an alternative to a language-based course in 'French'. Even where such options are in principle both open to any taker, it is a natural consequence of this kind of alternative that the groups will tend to constitute themselves roughly on the basis of ability in the subject. The school which offers a wider range of such alternatives will tend (independently of other variables) to create for itself relatively homogeneous groups; the school which insists by and large on a common curriculum will tend (again, other considerations apart) to

retain a relatively wide range of ability in any particular teach
ing group.

These five sets of considerations combine to demonstrate that
when we talk about a class being mixed ability we are talking
about a wide range of 'mixes'. There is an educationally
significant sense in which any group of children is a mixed
ability group. Indeed, this is precisely the point which many
advocates of mixed ability grouping want to make against those
who, they believe, treat streamed groups as an homogeneous
block. But clearly at the other extreme a particular combination
of circumstances and policies could generate groups of children
representing a range of ability that must surely defeat even the
most dogged refusal to recognise the variety of individual
needs.

Mixed Ability Teaching

It is one thing to decide to organise a school so that each class in
a given year group contains a full spectrum of ability (however
assessed). It is another thing to decide how to teach and how to
organise that group within the classroom. In our experience the
teachers most deeply disillusioned with mixed ability grouping
are those in schools which have taken the first of these steps
without giving proper consideration to the second. The recent
NFER study (Reid *et al.*, 1981) reported headteachers' views to
the effect that inflexibility in teaching methods represented one
of the major constraints on the effectiveness of mixed ability
grouping. As one head put it: 'We teach mixed ability groups
but we do not do mixed ability teaching.'

At the simplest level 'mixed ability teaching' is any mode of
teaching operated with a mixed ability class. In practice this can
mean a variety of strategies reflecting, among other things,
different views of the point or purpose of mixed ability grouping and its attendant educational and social values. These
include the following.

(a) *Undifferentiated Class Teaching*

Some teachers attempt to carry into the mixed ability class just the same style of class instruction which they had previously employed with a relatively homogeneous group, in spite of the obvious difficulties of matching the manner, pace and content of the instruction to the diverse levels of achievement among the children in their care.

(b) *Individual Work in Ability Groups*

A second, perhaps essentially conservative, response to mixed ability groups is to introduce a micro streaming structure within the classroom. In primary schools in particular this is commonly associated with the grouping of children around tables, each group working individually on assignments related to their approximate level of ability. Where resources permit, a remedial group, for example, may receive special help from a teacher with time set aside for this purpose.

(c) *Individualised Learning*

Some teachers judge that the only proper response to the variety of individual needs, which is made especially evident in mixed ability groups, is a programme of individually tailored assignments. Most often this involves the use (sometimes *ad nauseam!*) of commercially or personally produced workcards. The HMI report *Mixed Ability Work in Comprehensive Schools* (Department of Education and Science, 1978) reported that this was the most frequent alternative to whole class teaching encountered during the survey conducted by HMI. It argued, however, that distinction needed to be drawn between 'individual' work and 'individualised' work.

Individualised work involves personal assignments devised to meet the different needs, abilities and attainments of individual pupils. Individual work is activity on which the pupil is engaged by himself, at his own pace, but which is essentially the same as that being undertaken by the rest of the class. (p. 37)

The report adds that most of the work seen other than class

teaching was individual rather than individualised in the
which we are picking out here.

(d) *Collaborative Mixed Ability Group Work*

As we shall go on to explore in more detail (see Chapter 5
below), some teachers see a logical connection between a
preference for mixed ability grouping in the school and an
attraction to collaborative group work in the classroom. This
collaboration may be based on the allocation of tasks related to
different abilities (e.g. one child does the writing, a second
does the picture and a third pastes the two on to some card and
pins them on the wall). Alternatively, as with group discussion, team games, or choral singing, it can be based on the
deliberate suspension of such discrimination.

We are not at this stage concerned to be prescriptive as to
which or what combination of these or other teaching
strategies is most appropriate to mixed ability groups. For the
moment we wish merely to observe that 'mixed ability teaching' refers to a variety of teaching styles used with mixed
ability groups.

Ability

We have so far left unquestioned the ready assumption that
one of the things we have to take as given in contemplating
different forms of educational organisation is that children are
naturally distributed on some kind of hierarchy of ability
(which then provides a sensible basis for their distribution into
classes in school). This assumption is challenged by advocates
of mixed ability grouping in a number of ways.

One particular preoccupation which runs through much of
the discussion about the principles of comprehensive education as well as mixed ability teaching concerns the distinction
between attainment and potential. By 'attainment' is meant
something like presently demonstrable achievement or realised capacities; by 'potential' is meant some supposed capacity
which might have been realised by now had previous condi-

tions been more favourable or which could still be realised given the right conditions in the future. 'Ability' is a term which is used somewhat ambiguously to cover both attainment and potential.

Of course, empirical judgements about people's potential require inferences which rapidly become fairly conjectural. Deale has suggested that 'in practice we have *no* useful way of assessing potential (or even defining it) with regard to an individual child' (1977, p. 88). Daunt is more hopeful (1978, p. 54):

> Assessment of a child's potential is a difficult task, but not impossible. It involves, certainly, a comparison of past with present performance, but not only that, since obviously such a comparison could not on its own tell us anything about whether a child's whole recorded performance, both past and present, was comparatively good or bad in personal terms. Other data must therefore be collected to build up a picture of each child's potential. This must include observation of whether a child's performance is erratic, and if so in what ways; of the child's demeanour and attitude to work, including what the child says about the pleasure or frustration he experiences; of any known specific impediments to personal success, whether in the environment of home or school.

What is plainly the case, and this is a matter of logic which hardly requires empirical study, is that a child's potential cannot be established by mere mechanical comparison with present achievement. That a child cannot do something now implies neither that he could not have done it given more favourable circumstances hitherto nor that he could not do it given appropriate circumstances in the future. Part of the argument against streaming is that it creates conditions (including low expectations by pupils and teachers of likely achievement) which positively depress achievement in comparison with potential; part of the case in favour of mixed ability grouping is that it can remove at least this form of inhibition.

At the level of logical principle there are really rather few limits on what human beings in general or individual human beings, even those in the tenth stream, *might* not do, at least intellectually, in ideally adapted circumstances and in time. Not only this, but at the practical level it is sobering to reflect on the dramatic achievements of physically and mentally handicapped people for whom only a generation ago society would have had no higher ambition than they might through some mechanical skill contribute towards the cost of their own upkeep. Once we break out from our hidebound conceptions of when, where, in what conditions and with what human and technological assistance learning may go on, all sorts of new possibilities become open. As Jackson argues in one of the by now classical critiques of streaming (1964, p. 143):

> Excellence may have genetic limits, but we must alter circumstances a great deal before the genes finally stop our growth. Meanwhile our colossal technical resources can serve an imaginative approach to education, and rediscover what every great civilisation of the past stumbled on. In favourable circumstances, excellence is not static or severely limited. It multiplies.

The teacher who reports that a child 'could do better' is reporting a safe and almost logically necessary truth.

But what becomes particularly significant in the context of the egalitarian considerations which underlie some (though not all) of the arguments in favour of mixed ability grouping is that on this *a priori* argument we have no real reason to believe that the *potential* of the child who at present is a low achiever is necessarily less than that of the child who is at present a relatively high achiever. In any case the potential for both will almost certainly be both more varied and more extended than either will ever achieve. High on the list of human wastefulness is our unreadiness or inability to exploit the full richness of our own human talents.

Not that we could or should wish to develop all human potentials equally. We have potentials which we may regard as destructive or evil and which we may seek to curb. We have potentials (e.g. for artistic invention) which we might very well value more than others (e.g. waggling one's ears). We have potentials (e.g. for weight-lifting and long-distance running) whose pursuit makes conflicting demands on our time and our nature. The school that declares its aims as being 'to develop the fullest potential' of the children is obscuring the inevitable choices which have to be made in terms of the potentials which it will seek to develop and those it will not.

However, the points remain that within that range of potentials which we do seek to develop in schools, first, the potential for any child is not commensurate with his achievement and secondly, somewhat more speculatively, the gap between the potential and achievement of any one child is probably significantly greater than the gap between the achievement of one child and another.

We are not sure how this last conviction could be either established or refuted empirically. For the moment we can only record that it seems to be a significant article of faith among those who regard observable differences of attainment as indicators rather of relatively favourable or unfavourable socio-educational circumstances than of significant differences in personal capacity. Thus Crosland (1962, p. 173) argued (in phrases closely echoed by Sir Edward Boyle in his preface to the Newsom Report one year later): 'we have failed to create a social environment in which all children in their early years have an equal chance of acquiring measured intelligence, so far as this can be controlled by social action'.

2

The Rationale

In this chapter we shall be concerned to articulate and comment on what we see as the central arguments used by teachers and others in education in defence of mixed ability grouping. We recognise that this account must rest in part on empirical studies of what teachers actually say about their reasons, and to this end we shall be drawing on published surveys and case studies. But we shall at the same time try to give fuller articulation to arguments which receive somewhat fragmentary expression in the literature and, in conclusion, to comment on some of their implications and internal contradictions. We shall set out in the following four sections four arguments or sets of arguments which seem to us to have some rather distinctive features.

(1) The Better To Select You By

Red Riding Hood mixed ability lives kinder and more thorough than the examinatorial wolf: 'What a lot of mixed ability you've got in the first year, headmaster.' 'All the better to *set* them with, later, my child?' (Davies, 1977, p. 31)

Let us acknowledge first of all that schools (or more particularly secondary schools) have one interest in mixed ability grouping which is essentially conservative in character. What such schools are concerned to establish is essentially a more

11

sophisticated and perhaps fairer version of the old system of selection. Their pupils will rapidly move into streamed or setted groups but are placed in mixed ability groups for perhaps the first year so as to enable the school to make up its own mind about their abilities on the basis of sustained observation and the school's own tests. In theory at least the child is allowed to enter the competition with 'a clean slate', that is, he can put behind the disadvantages of past failure (as also, of course, the advantages of past success). Reid *et al.* (1981) observed that this desire to give children a fresh start 'and to avoid labelling' at the outset of a child's secondary career was in fact by far the most common reason cited in its favour by heads who were in office when their schools introduced mixed ability grouping. It came top too among teachers' perceptions of the advantages of mixed ability grouping in this NFER study.

One dimension of this argument is the reluctance of secondary schools to place much reliance on the judgements made by their 'feeder' primary schools about their pupils' abilities. The study by the ILEA Inspectorate (1976) referred to the opinion of many secondary teachers that 'There is no clear correlation between primary school assessment and performance in the secondary school, and streamed or banded groupings based on a series of tests shortly after arrival at the secondary school would be suspect' (p. 14). Reid *et al.* (1981) refer similarly to 'the "known" inaccuracy of predictive tests' and quote the opinion of one headteacher that 'There wasn't enough information from primary schools to stream; in any case we didn't want to act on others' information' (p. 26). Davies (1977) gives a parallel example of someone he describes as a very experienced head in a comprehensive school with an intake strongly unbalanced towards the low-ability side, who thought: 'You can no longer rely on what in my time we called the mechanics of primary education . . . That being so, I think that until they acquire the mechanics and come to see what they are being used for, it is rather wrong to label them in any special way on their arrival at school' (p. 28).

These opinions invite, and indeed already have been subject to, a number of observations. Reid and her colleagues were prompted to ask, for example: 'What are secondary teachers

12

really saying about the professionalism of their primary colleagues when they assert that they do not wish to accept "others'" judgement of pupils?' (p. 27) However, whatever condescension is or is not implied in the sentiments of secondary teachers, there are obvious practical difficulties involved in ensuring that the criteria against which a particular secondary school seeks to assess pupils accord with those of one primary, let alone the dozen or more that may feed a secondary school in a rural area or in an urban setting in which parents enjoy a wide degree of choice of school. Some groups of schools have gone a long way in developing a consensus around these criteria, but this is by no means universal practice. Meanwhile, one feature of the kind of 'professionalism' espoused by teachers in England and Wales is the degree of autonomy enjoyed by individual schools in the establishment of teaching objectives and hence criteria of assessment.

The second question posed in the NFER report (Reid *et al.*, 1981) concerns the concept of the 'fresh start'. How realistic is it to talk of children at the age of 11 having a 'fresh start' in their education? Again, what sort of a judgement is implied on the first six years of their schooling if their achievements or failings during this period are somehow supposed to be ignored? Different kinds of skill, knowledge and understanding will have been acquired. Different curricula will have been followed. Some will have one or two years' experience in French, science, computing; some will have none. Some will have done the Tudors to death, others will know nothing of history after the motte and bailey castle. Surely it is neither practicable nor desirable for a secondary teacher to ignore all this? Nor is it possible for children entering the secondary school to do so without the advantage or disadvantage of achievements drawn from their primary experience. The start can be 'fresh' only in the sense that the secondary teacher tries to allow children to demonstrate their strengths and weaknesses themselves rather than to come to the new school already 'labelled' by ('accompanied by the careful assessment of'?) their primary teachers. But this takes us back to some of the issues already indicated.

The expressed concern for a 'fresh start' at 11 embodies nevertheless an important principle which we shall see developed more fully in some of the other arguments in favour of mixed ability grouping. It seems to represent at least a rather restricted version of the principle of justice or equality of opportunity. This kind of concern for justice or equality is fully compatible with a meritocratic and hierarchical social order in which goods are eventually distributed unequally in some sort of reflection of a pyramid-like structure of achievement. The principle of equality is applied in this context to ensure what is thought to be a fair or just competition for these social goods, and 'fairness' or 'justice' consists in ensuring that competitors start at some stage on what is seen as an equal footing – they have the same starting line. Now part of what teachers seem to be saying when they advocate a 'fresh start' at 11, mixed ability groups in the first year of secondary education, assessment and then streaming, is: 'The starting line is here! We shall treat you for twelve months without prejudice. Only on the basis of achievements which you demonstrate in that time will we make judgements about your ability and hence the curriculum and pace of work which you will follow henceforth.' At least this is what *seems* to be implied in this kind of practice and in what teachers say about it.

Again, however, we have to note that even if teachers remove in this way what might be one handicap in the competition, misleading or prejudicial assessments by former teachers, they are certainly not removing all relevant advantages or disadvantages which have accrued from birth and before. If opportunity is made dependent upon achievement, equality of opportunity can only seriously be available where equality of achievement already exists.

Moreover, what is not clear is why some of those who are so anxious about 'labelling', 'self-fulfilling prophecies', 'the halo effect' and 'writing children off' at 11 are so ready to accept these consequences of assessment and streaming at 12 or 13. As we shall go on to see, some of those who advocate the postponement of any kind of selective grouping are concerned to put off for as long as possible the start of the race, to reduce perhaps the gap between the least and the most advantaged by the time of that start and even to dissociate as far as possible the business of education from the selection of young people for their different places in the social hierarchy. That this is a

14

headier kind of egalitarianism than anything with which advocates of the diagnostic year of mixed ability grouping would normally choose to be associated is clear. *Why* they do not see it as a logical conclusion of their concern about avoiding labelling, allowing fresh starts and ensuring fair competition is less so.

(2) Avoiding Some of the Worst Consequences of Streaming

> There is no dreaded 2c. (Head of department, quoted in ILEA Inspectorate, 1976)

For many teachers the move to mixed ability grouping was not inspired by any very lofty social ideals but was a relatively pragmatic response to the immediate problem created by the reactions of groups of lower stream pupils for whom school represented a constant and humiliating reminder of what in educational terms had come to be defined as their own inadequacy or inferiority. 'The great common denominator', writes Davies, 'is a desire to get away from the worst features of streaming. These are most sharply focussed upon as the production of demoralized, demotivated, unteachable middle-school groups, bad for themselves, their teachers and other children' (1977, p. 27). The ILEA survey reported that all the schools in its sample referred to this factor. 'Elitist groups on the one hand produce "sink" groups on the other', explained one headteacher (ILEA Inspectorate, 1976). Similarly, the HMI study gave this as one of the main arguments offered in favour of mixed ability grouping (Department of Education and Science, 1978, p. 17):

> Pupils difficult to handle would be dispersed instead of being kept together to form anti-social groups. Undesirable feelings such as inferiority, superiority or aggression, and undesirable attitudes such as competitiveness, would tend to diminish, as would tensions between pupils and teachers. More cooperative behaviour would be developed, and good order maintained. Self

esteem, security and self reliance would be encouraged, as would good relationships among pupils and between pupils and teachers.

At its simplest, then, mixed ability grouping may be seen as a means of dispersing rather than concentrating together those pupils whose failure (in school terms) is most likely to lead them into disillusionment and thence into disruptive behaviour. At very least this might make them easier to contain; at best it may help to avoid them developing a view of themselves, or avoid teachers too clearly identifying them, as the 'sink' of the school.

The kind of optimism reflected in this argument is based in part on the judgement that the institutional arrangements might themselves be conducive to the sense of failure and frustration experienced by many less able pupils. We have already referred to the prominence given in responses to the NFER survey to teachers' concern to avoid the consequences of 'labelling' children. Research findings indicating the way in which children's own acceptance of a low ability identity, or teachers' acceptance of it in relation to a child, can operate as a self-fulfilling prophecy seem to have become established wisdom among teachers. Many teachers acknowledge too that lower streams in secondary schools have commonly been disadvantaged in terms of resources and facilities and taught by teachers, who, if they were not in fact inferior to their colleagues, often came to feel that they were. The 'less able' seemed to lose out all ways round.

On some views this social-psychological analysis needs to be located within a broader sociological framework, though we have to acknowledge that teachers offering such analysis do not appear to be sufficiently numerous to feature centrally in the recent ILEA, HMI, or NFER surveys (either that or surveys do not encourage teachers to articulate more systematic and radical analyses of educational experience?). Briefly, and no doubt oversimplistically, what this broader argument draws attention to is the tendency of streaming structures in schools to reinforce the vicious circle of social-economic disadvantage → educational disadvantage → educational failure → social-economic disadvantage.

16

Those who offer such analyses are rarely optimistic th
cycle can be broken simply by educational change. I
studies like Stephen Ball's fascinating account of the c___
over to mixed ability grouping at Beechside Comprehensive
are cited as examples of the way in which underlying structures are untouched by attempts at institutional change. 'The
most striking aspect of the analysis of the mixed ability forms
in this study is the absence of dramatic change' (Ball, 1981, p.
285). Nevertheless, they help to locate more specific discussion of the merits of streaming within the context of wider
questions of social justice and injustice and remind us again
that however practical or 'pragmatic' we try to be about
grouping in schools, fundamental questions about social justice lie not far below the surface.

(3) Respecting Each Child as an Individual of Equal Worth

Mixed ability teaching takes place when a teacher tries to
regulate his treatment of individual differences by the
principle of equality. (Elliott, 1976, p. 4)

One important argument in support of mixed ability grouping
is based on the principle of equal respect for each child as an
individual. One thread of this argument suggests that when we
have streamed, banded, or setted classes we tend to rely on the
process of selection to give us relatively homogeneous groups
and thence to treat them as a block. As the ILEA report put it
(1976, p. 15):

Streaming or banding merely disguises and ignores differences in abilities and rates of progress and equally
presents the problems (often unrecognised) of stretching
the brightest pupils and maintaining the understanding
of the less able in the class. Mixed ability classes force
teachers to recognise these problems.

Many of the comments made by teachers reflect the supposi-
tion that if you are teaching a mixed ability group you cannot
help but recognise the range of different individual needs.

17

Daunt, for example, in perhaps the most eloquent and developed defence of the comprehensive principle (and thence directly and indirectly of mixed ability grouping), suggests that while 'the teacher of the streamed class or set is inclined to perceive the individual through the group .. through the fiction (on which streaming and setting depend) that the group is significantly homogeneous', the teacher of the mixed ability class 'is impelled to advance the authenticity of his knowledge and understanding of individual children and to promote individual learning as one of his predominant methods' (Daunt, 1975, p. 55). One of the teachers interviewed in connection with the NFER survey reported: 'I grew up and expanded as a teacher because I was thrust into talking face to face rather than as a class' (Reid *et al.*, 1981, p. 74).

This respect for the individual child has in some teachers' minds far-reaching implications for school organisation. The HMI survey, for example, starts with reference to the objection to the *classification* of children and thence their *streaming* and *ranking*. But it goes on to refer to teachers' expectations that '*curricula* differentiated by ability would be avoided' and that 'mixed ability grouping would promote the matching of *individual programmes* to individual needs . . . the *allocation of the oldest teachers* to the ablest pupils . . . would be avoided . . . they would be obliged to avoid uniform, whole-class teaching . . . new styles of learning, including small group and *individual learning techniques*, would be encouraged . . . *resources for learning* would have to be more diverse . . . *continuity with primary school styles* would be ensured'; '*assessment* of each pupil against his own potential would be encouraged' (Department of Education and Science, 1978, p. 18; our italics).

What these aspirations indicate is something of the strength of the commitment to respect for the individual and individual differences which lies behind at least some people's espousal of the cause of mixed ability grouping – sentiments summarised perhaps in Caulfield's explanation of teachers' reasons for introducing mixed ability teaching at Bishop Douglass school (1977, p. 74):

Our conviction rested on the simple conclusion that children even of the same family are human beings of different abilities, personalities and characters. We would argue that mixed ability teaching is a recognition of this individuality because the essence of the methodology is teaching the individual child and satisfying his educational needs.

One interesting feature of Caulfield's argument, however, is his explicit disavowal of egalitarian concerns which others see as inextricably associated with this concern for individual development. 'We would have been astonished if anyone had thought we were engaged in egalitarianism or social engineering' (p. 74). Other writers in the individualist tradition, howeVer, clearly recognise the importance of combining with the concern for the individual a principle requiring the equal distribution of that concern, respect, or value. Thus Elliott sees the teacher in the mixed ability class as seeking 'to regulate his treatment of individual differences by the principle of equality' (1976, p. 4). Similarly Daunt presents the kind of teacher who properly embodies the spirit of comprehensive schooling in these terms (1975, p. 15):

> He is egalitarian, not in the absurd sense of believing that all talents and aptitudes are equal, but yet in a stronger sense than merely advocating . . . equality of opportunity: he wishes to see all members of society equally valued.

The HMI survey makes similar reference in these terms (Department of Education and Science, 1978, p. 17)

> Mixed ability grouping would prevent the rejection of the less able implied in streaming, setting or banding; would tend to avoid putting pupils into rank order; or would even enable the avoidance of any classification of pupils at all. The equal value of all individuals would thereby be demonstrated, and there would be equality of opportunity, or equality as such, for all.

What we seem to be presented with here, then, is a principle which would allow or even encourage different children to follow different curricula, in different ways at different paces.

(It would thus contrast with other principles which underlie defences of mixed ability teaching which link the practice with a common curriculum and common objectives.) But the principle is egalitarian in the sense that it demands equal concern, attention, respect and value for all children and (which may be more difficult to command) for what they do.

(4) Expressing and Encouraging the Values of Fraternity, Community and Co-operation

Aspirations such as improvement in human relationships or social integration were more frequently cited than, for example, such aims as improving the attainment of the less able pupils. (Department of Education and Science, 1978, p. 15)

The more recent NFER survey confirms the observation reported here that teachers attach considerable importance to the social benefits of mixed ability grouping, but it notes too that the nature of these advantages was frequently not articulated. The phrase "the usual social advantages" was employed by many teachers in their interview and this unquestioning expression of social benefits was reflected in an almost total lack of interest in exploring the social outcomes of mixed ability teaching in the subsequent group discussions (Reid *et al.*, 1981, p. 73).

There are, however, a sufficient number of phrases which recur in teachers' comments about these social advantages to give us some picture of their character. Reid's own report recorded references to children 'all getting on well together, respecting each other's individual differences and each other's work' and the suggestion that this led to 'an increase in tolerance of individual foibles within the group'. Mixed ability groups were valued for the 'concrete example' they provided of what some teachers believed to be the philosophy of the real world – 'showing that each person has something to offer'. By comparison, teachers working in streamed classes referred to this system as 'socially divisive' (ibid., pp. 72, 73). Among the arguments cited in the HMI survey are prominent references to the opinion that 'mixed ability grouping would help to counteract class differences, and would work against the continuance of a competitive, elitist and divided society'. This form of grouping was believed to encourage 'social integration and a sense of community'. And later, 'pupils would learn to help each other' (Department of Education and Science, 1978, p. 17).

The social values or principles which underlie these and other similar references (see e.g. E. M. Hoyles' account of mixed ability grouping at Vauxhall Manor school in Kelly, 1975) seem to be distinguishable from the concerns to which we have so far referred. The fathers of the French Revolution were clear-minded enough to distinguish two principles which later social theorists and some advocates of mixed ability teaching have tended to blur. We refer to the principles of 'equality' and 'fraternity'. One thread of the argument in support of mixed ability grouping is opposed to the institutionalised segregation of different sections of the population not only because this is instrumentally associated with inequality but because it is itself intrinsically undesirable. The ideal society on this view is a community (a commune?) which is at least relatively unhierarchical in character; in which there is mutuality of concern and respect, and co-operation in the pursuit of collective and individual good; in which there is a willing acceptance of the principle that no individual or group interest will persistently be subordinated to another – for all of which a certain kind of equality of consideration will be a necessary but not a sufficient condition.

Anthony Crosland observed and amplified the importance of the principle of fraternity (though he did not use this term) in his seminal essay 'Comprehensive education' (1974, p. 204):

Now by selecting for a superior school children who are already well favoured by environment, we are not merely confirming, we are hardening and sharpening, an existing social division. This can surely not be thought desirable. I will not argue the point in terms of equality. But I will argue it in terms of a sense of community, of social cohesion, of a nation composed of people who understand each other because they can communicate. If the only

21

time we can, as a society, achieve this common language is when we go to war, than we are at a much less advanced stage than many societies which the anthropologists describe as primitive. We have only to consider our industrial relations, and the lack of communication and mutual understanding reflected in them, to see the depth of social division in Britain today. Of course, education alone cannot solve this problem. But so long as we choose to educate our children in separate camps, reinforcing and seeming to validate existing differences in accent, language and values, for so long will our schools exacerbate rather than diminish our class divisions.

Crosland went on to draw explicitly the implication that the considerations which applied to the elimination of separatism in schooling applied equally to separatism within a school (p. 204):

Of course the elimination of separatism at 11-plus is only a necessary, and not a sufficient, condition of reducing the divisive effect of our school system. We should not much improve matters if selection gave way merely to rigid streaming within a strictly neighbourhood pattern of schools. This would re-create many of the old evils within a comprehensive system.

Thus the talk, perhaps the rhetoric, of mixed ability teaching offers a picture of a (closely interrelated) set of social values which mixed ability grouping is expected to reinforce:

social integration
social cohesion
community
mutual understanding
mutual respect
mutual support
tolerance
co-operation
equality

and of their negation:

22

segregation
separatism
social divisiveness
the absence of mutual understanding, respect and support
intolerance
competitiveness
inequality.

It is the positive set of values which we take, roughly speaking, to be represented by or rooted in the traditional notion of 'fraternity'.

Summary, Some Distinctions and Some Problems

We have largely, though not exclusively, restricted ourselves so far to articulating some of the many arguments which seem to underlie teachers' support for mixed ability grouping. On our analysis they are rooted in one or more of the following principles or concerns:

justice or equality of opportunity in a weaker sense applied as a principle governing discrimination between courses and teaching styles in an (eventually) streamed school, and governing access to those streams;

justice or equality of opportunity in a stronger sense applied as a principle governing children's capacity to compete for social (including further educational) advantages when they leave school – implying within practical limits an attempt to enable children to secure the same kind of educational advantages while they are at school (and hence approximating to the more radical egalitarian goal of equality of achievement);

equality of respect (or value) for individuals, in which the principle of equality is invoked as a distributive principle governing the value which is to be placed on every individual and attempts to develop them, in all their diversity;

fraternity, which extends the principle of equality of respect

23

into a representation of an integrated, mutually supportive, interactive community.

Before we go on to look more closely at the nature and justification of some of these principles let us note certain features
of the argument(s) so far expressed.

First, people often try to contrast what they call the 'educational' arguments in favour of mixed ability teaching with
the 'social' arguments. The HMI report acknowledged the
difficulty and to some extent the falseness of this distinction
and then proved the case by getting into some confusion when
it tried nevertheless to operate with the distinction. In our
view, and this is well illustrated in the presentation of arguments in this chapter, identifiable social principles or values
underlie all the major arguments in support of mixed ability
grouping.

Our second observation, however, and this is easily supported again by reference to the preceding arguments, is that the
social principles referred to in support of mixed ability teaching are not all of a kind and are not even compatible. They
represent some distinctive and on the face of it conflicting
concerns. There is a conflict, for example, between the principle that calls merely for a fair competition in school for
educational success and hence (it is assumed) social advantage
and the principle which requires schools to establish the conditions under which a more equal competition for social
advantage can take place once children have left schools.
There is a *prima facie* conflict (as the HMI survey itself observed) between the concern for individuality and the concern for
equality. 'The notion of equality tends to be associated with a
common curriculum and common provision to which all must
have equal access, that of individuality is associated with
variety and divergence' (Department of Education and
Science, 1978, pp. 18–19).

Similarly, and again this point is made by HMI, it is not
easy to reconcile the aims of social and intellectual integration
with that of each child pursuing his own goals, the groupy
gregariousness of the commune with the private space and
quiet self-examination which seem to belong with the cultiva-
tion of the self-sufficient individual.

If it is possible to resolve some of these apparent conflicts, they serve nevertheless to warn us that the case in favour of mixed ability teaching is by no means all of a piece.

Our third observation follows from the first two, for it is clear that the different arguments in favour of mixed ability teaching have some rather different consequences for the organisation of mixed ability teaching in practice. In particular, as David Bridges has already argued elsewhere (Bridges, 1976), the arguments seem to have different implications for the teaching of mixed ability groups in the classroom. Where mixed ability grouping is seen as having a largely diagnostic function it may be quite compatible with class teaching which allows an individual response that indicates the relative capacities of the group of children in question. (Though let us be clear that few serious advocates of the intrinsic merits of mixed ability teaching would defend this kind of practice.) For others who stress the principle of equal value or concern for each individual pupil, as we have already seen, mixed ability teaching is inextricably associated with individualised learning (i.e. differentiated programmes of work tailored specifically to individual needs). For others again, the concern to encourage social and intellectual contact and integration, understanding of individual differences, mutual respect and co-operation suggests the suitability of group projects, group discussion, or team work of one kind or another.

Similarly, there is what the HMI report regarded as the most difficult division of principle and practice – and this concerns attitudes towards assessment. Some of the arguments which (perhaps somewhat contortedly?) oppose any kind of assessment on the grounds that this is bound to be unfair, that the subsequent 'labelling' is prejudicial to the less able, or that any such assessment is essentially dehumanising are difficult to reconcile with the concern which underlies other advocacies of mixed ability teaching, to match curriculum teaching style and/or resources to individual needs. How such matching is to be done without *some* form of assessment is difficult to understand.

These differences in the practical implications of the arguments we have picked out go to support the view that there are some significant differences between the arguments themselves.

Conclusion

What we have done so far is to illustrate the way in which people have begun to justify an educational practice by reference to certain social principles. We have also shown certain tensions between the social principles invoked, such that it is difficult to see that they can be deployed in consort, so to speak, in support of mixed ability teaching. An adequate justification would have to rely on one or some of these arguments rather than the whole package.

Apart from this, however, there are other conditions which would need to be satisfied before we could claim to have an adequate justification for mixed ability teaching. It is by no means enough to display a kind of *prima facie* symmetry between the educational practice and the social principles referred to.

In particular we shall need to ask two questions. First, the question resolvable (in principle) by reference to further empirical evidence: *does the practice (mixed ability grouping) have in fact the desirable consequences (equality, fraternity, etc.) which it is hoped to have?* Secondly, the question which invites closer philosophical scrutiny: *are the social principles by reference to which the practice is justified (in particular equality and fraternity) themselves coherent and justifiable?* We shall not in this book, which is concerned with the social philosophy of mixed ability teaching, say very much about the empirical evidence – though we shall want to return to this at least briefly in Chapter 6 below. In the next two chapters, however, we shall comment in more detail on the philosophical arguments underlying the principles of equality and fraternity.

3

Justice and Equality

In Chapter 2 we noted that different views of mixed ability grouping can often be seen to reflect attachment to different social principles, particularly to principles of justice and equality. In this chapter the intention is to examine rather more closely ideas of justice and equality and to see if any justifiable connection can be made between justice and/or equality on the one hand and mixed ability grouping on the other. The word 'justifiable' is worth emphasising since we do not find the problem of justification normally pursued as far as it might be in the available literature discussing possible rationales for mixed ability grouping. It is one thing to note, as we have done, the various ways in which views about mixed ability grouping appear to be rooted in ideas of justice and equality; it is quite another thing to present justifications for either the connections or the underlying ideas, and when such justificatory arguments are offered they are sometimes rather weak.

An example of such a weak argument, offered as a positive rationale for mixed ability grouping, is to be found in a book by A. V. Kelly (1978). After rehearsing rather familiar arguments demonstrating the faults of streaming, which constitute for him a negative case for mixed ability grouping, he goes on to construct a positive rationale 'by reference to the changed and changing needs and ideology of both education and society'. It is reasonably clear, however, that this kind of argument, which takes it for granted that educational practice must simply reflect observable ideological changes in society, will not do the justificatory job it claims to do. Such arguments simply analyse, more or less correctly, ideological change and attempt to show what kind of educational arrangements best suit such changes. They avoid entering the difficult area of argument about values presupposed in the ideologies discussed and therefore fail to provide any kind of real justification for the practices supported. We cannot, therefore, sympathise with these attempts to provide a rationale for mixed ability grouping.

Some attempts have been made, however, to connect an underlying and presumably absolute value principle, which is not merely a part of an ideology, with mixed ability grouping. An instructive example, which we have already noted, comes from P. E. Daunt in asserting his Comprehensive Principle which claims that 'the education of all children is held to be intrinsically of equal value' (Daunt, 1975, p. 16). As indicated in the last chapter, this is one of the main ideas of equality and justice that teachers seem to have in mind when favouring mixed ability grouping – namely, respecting each child as an individual of equal worth.

Now if such a principle is sound then certainly there are implications arising from it for mixed ability grouping, as we shall try to show later in this chapter. Unfortunately, however, although Daunt has extremely interesting things to say about the working out of this principle in the policy-making and teaching arrangements of comprehensive schools, and although he relates the principle very specifically to mixed ability grouping, he does not seem very confident in the grounding or justification of the principle itself. Indeed, he says 'clearly it would be perfectly possible rationally to reject the principle altogether ... perfectly possible, too, to substitute a different principle' (ibid., p. 16). If this is so, one is bound to ask why anyone should accept the principle or urge it upon others. Daunt himself sees the principle as a 'genuinely uncontaminated corollary' of his aims of education, which he gives as helping a person to

1(a) understand himself   1(b) improve himself
2(a) understand his total   2(b) improve his relations
     environment   with his environment

but he appears equally unclear as to whether we are to take these aims as self-evident or not; and what it actually means for the principle to be a 'genuinely uncontaminated corollary' of such aims is certainly not obvious. However much we might like the principle – and we do – the justificatory account remains to be given.

Suppose it to be asserted that children should be taught in mixed ability groups because it is more just than grouping them in any other way. To know whether the justification part of this claim is meaningful and really does constitute a justification or not we need to look at the idea of justice, and in looking at this idea we shall inevitably be looking at the idea of equality as well. The kind of justice and equality that we are concerned with in this context is to do with the treatment of persons by other persons: in this particular case the treatment of persons who are pupils by other persons who are teachers or school administrators. We need to ask whether there are any general and fundamental rules by which we can decide what is just, fair, or equitable treatment, and what is not.

The first view to dispose of, necessarily so because even ministers of education still use it (Boyson, 1981), is the idea that egalitarians believe justice to lie in the exactly equal treatment of all people because people are exactly equal in all respects. This view is such patent nonsense that it enables non-egalitarians like Rhodes Boyson to reject egalitarianism without more ado. The truth, of course, is that this view *is* nonsense and bears no resemblance to what egalitarians actually say. They might say that all people are equal in certain respects, but that is a different argument, certainly not nonsense, which we shall come to in due course. For the time being let us be quite clear that it is *not* just to treat pupils as though they are exactly alike. Indeed, to do so would be unjust, as we have realised at least since the time of Aristotle. Defenders of mixed ability grouping cannot, and as far as we know do not try to, ground their case here.

To treat people justly, equally, or fairly you do not have to treat them exactly alike. Justice does not require this, but it does require two other important things: first, that if people *are* the same in important respects then they should be

29

treated the same in so far as the treatment bears on those respects; and, secondly, that differences of treatments should be appropriately connected with some relevant differences to be found in the people concerned. The important point here is that in a number of cases differential treatment, providing one kind of thing for some people and different kinds of things for others, is *exactly* what fairness or justice demands. Difference of provision, treatment or allocation of resources is never in itself evidence of injustice. We always need to ask further questions about the nature of the differences and the relevance of those differences to the differences of treatment or provision before we can judge about possible injustice.

This idea of distributive justice or fairness relates to Daunt's idea of the equal value of education for all children because here education is seen as a 'good' of which some persons could conceivably have more than others in terms of allocated resources, time spent in education, access to good teachers, and so on. The way education is shared out and organised is a problem of distributive justice. Education is particularly a problem of distributive justice because it is widely held by modern political, social and moral philosophers to constitute what is called a *primary* good. All sorts of things can be goods – for instance, things people might desire – but some things are necessary in a much stronger sense than just being wanted. Such goods are necessary in the sense that a person *must* have them in order to operate, now or eventually, as a purposive agent, that is, 'one capable of fulfilling purposes through action' (Gewirth, 1978, p. 244) and such things are usefully called primary goods. Most writers on these matters either include education as a primary good or see education as necessarily related to primary goods like freedom, knowledge, or self-esteem. Alan Gewirth, for example, in his book *Reason and Morality*, argues that both knowledge and freedom are necessities of what he calls 'unforced choice' and 'for the achievement of both knowledge and freedom education is a prime means' (ibid., p. 245).

A further example of this kind of underlying moral argument is to be found in John Rawls's influential work *A Theory* of Justice (1972). Rawls talks of the essential primary good of self-respect and goes on to argue (p. 107):

> It follows that the confident sense of their own worth should be sought for the least favored and this limits the forms of hierarchy and degrees of inequality that justice permits. Thus, for example, resources for education are not to be allocated solely or necessarily mainly according to their return as estimated in productive trained abilities, but also according to their worth in enriching the personal and social life of citizens, including here the least favored.

What follows from these kinds of argument is indeed something like Daunt's principle of the equal value of education to all children, but we now have the strong supporting basis that this is an equal right to children as persons, as human agents, quite irrespective of variations in ability or other characteristics of personality. The basic claim to equality of educational provision in some sense is therefore a strong one and not to be dismissed by pointing to the undeniable differences that exist among pupils.

We must note, too, that the claim here is to *equality* of treatment and provision, and not just to the idea of *equality of opportunity* that has been so fashionable a conception in educational discussion. In Chapter 2 we noted both a weak and a strong sense of equality of opportunity discernible in some advocacy of mixed ability grouping. The weaker sense embodies the idea of giving children an equal chance to enter an essentially unequal system – a streamed school – by, say, enabling differences to emerge in a relatively short-lived mixed ability period. The stronger sense sees the period of equal treatment as extending throughout school so as to give the pupil an equal opportunity to cope with the unequal life struggle after school. The idea of equality of opportunity has been examined and criticised in a number of ways in recent years and it is now difficult to see how the notion can adequately serve an appropriately moral treatment of pupils in any continuous sense as actual or potential purposive agents. Rawls, for example, links the idea of equality of opportunity

31

with the idea of a meritocratic society, lacking in fraternity, and sees it as giving people 'an equal chance to leave behind the less fortunate in the personal quest for influence and social position' (ibid., pp. 106–7). Rawls himself, of course, propounds a principle of social justice in which differences, inequalities, in the provision of goods are only to be justified if such differences make the least well off better off than they would have been without the differences. Such a principle, in practice, would help to produce fraternity by means of its patent justice and non-arbitrariness. More to our present point, perhaps, is the fact that such a principle is rarely satisfied where differences of educational treatment or provision are very pronounced. It would have to be shown, on this argument, that the least well off pupils *educationally* gain more by the existence of differences of educational provision and treatment than they would by the absence of such differences.

Other writers (Daunt, 1975; Williams, 1969) have pointed out the oddness of the notion of equality of opportunity, noting its concern to give equal chances to achieve unequal and necessarily limited rewards, as in a handicap race. Daunt points out that in the educational context, all too often, the alleged equality of opportunity is offered once only, as in the 11-plus selection procedure, after which all the evidence indicates an increasing lack of opportunity for the least well off. The more the actual equality of treatment extends throughout the pupil's school life, as in the stronger of our two senses, then the less of a distinction there is for educational purposes between equality *per se* and equality of opportunity. In any case, what is being talked about here, in an attempt to provide an underpinning justification for mixed ability grouping in terms of social justice, is not equality of opportunity, but rather some more ongoing and continuous form of equality of treatment and provision based on the idea of every pupil's claim to be treated as an actual or potential purposive agent who can only act as such if able to receive his or her fair share of primary goods which would include education. We must now consider whether a preference for mixed ability grouping necessarily follows from this kind of principle.

In trying to relate ideas about the grouping of pupils to

principles of distributive justice there are two difficulties to deal with. First, there is the difficulty of determining what would constitute the *same* treatment of provision in terms of grouping. This is necessary because we have to know what *does* constitute sameness of treatment or provision before we can investigate, secondly, what might constitute good and relevant reasons for deviating from it in some cases, few or many. It is thus well worth asking what kind of grouping would form a kind of datum sameness-of-treatment grouping of pupils in school if there were no question of treating any of them differently. To avoid complications that are probably unrealistic we shall assume that we are talking about arrangements of groups within overall year-groups of roughly comparable age.

A useful heuristic device here is to imagine something like the state of ignorance posited by Rawls – that is, to imagine a group of rational agents ignorant of what actual differences of ability, intelligence and personality they might have, but knowing that they were to be grouped for learning and desirious of finding the most rational principles for such grouping. What this device does, in effect, is to make clear that the only characteristic of the individuals to be grouped that should be considered, in the first instance at least, is the characteristic of purposive agency which all persons have in common. Now such persons would not wish, could not rationally wish, special characteristics such as high intelligence, convergent thinking, or special abilities to be specially valued in such groupings as may be made, since they would not know whether, in particular cases, they would have these characteristics. To group according to ability, specific or general, is to group according to variable characteristics other than the non-variable characteristic of purposive agency and would necessarily be rejected as a rational principle for grouping for sameness of treatment. The only way in which initial sameness of treatment can be accorded, and equal valuing plainly be signalled, is for *each person to be in a group which is as mixed in terms of abilities as any other group that he/she could be in*.

Some have argued, Daunt for example, that not only does such a principle of mixed ability grouping establish this kind of datum – a basic sameness, deviations from which have to be justified in order to satisfy a principle of distributive justice – but it ensures a kind of equal valuing of pupils as purposive individuals in a much more substantive sense:

> The teacher of a mixed ability class is impelled to advance the authenticity of his knowledge and understanding of individual children and to promote individual learning as one of his predominant methods. The teacher of the streamed class or set is inclined to perceive the individual through the group, and therefore to stress an inter-personal excellence, through the fiction (on which streaming and setting depend) that the group is significantly homogeneous; he is moreover committed to a system of promotions and demotions which require yet further emphasis on interpersonal success. (Daunt, 1975, p. 55)

We encounter here again the mixture of empirical expectations and claimed logical connections characteristic of much educational discussion. Teachers do not, of course, *necessarily* teach mixed ability groups by individual methods, though perhaps they should, since we often see such groups being taught *as if* they were homogeneous as to abilities and other characteristics. Some teachers *do* give a great deal of individual instruction and concern even in streamed and setted groups. Nevertheless, there is strength in Daunt's arguments: the connection between setting and streaming and a system of promotions and demotions *does* appear to be a logical connection in that the latter would have no point without the former; and promotions and demotions, however glossed, imply a valuing of what one is promoted to and a devaluing of what one is promoted from, to say nothing of demotions. It does also seem to be the case that mixed ability grouping presents individual teachers with the appropriate social justice question in a way that neither streaming nor setting does – that question being: 'Given that these children are put into a mixed ability group as of equal value, what individual differences that they might have are relevant to differences of educational treatment that I might provide?' In setting or streaming situations the assumption is always that the social justice question has already been dealt with in the grouping arrangements, and the teacher can assume a homogeneous group in the respects relevant to his teaching.

Our conclusion must be, then, that the appropriate datum, the position from which questions about relevant differences must start, is the mixed ability group, where 'mixed ability group' means not simply an ignoring of differences of ability but a deliberate mixing to ensure that all children work together in groups mixed in the same way as all other groups. It is important to emphasise that the establishing of this datum is nothing to do with teaching efficiency or teacher convenience but everything to do with *the patent demonstration of the equal valuing of education for every pupil considered as a purposive agent.*

This brings us to our second difficulty: the establishing of the datum of what sameness of treatment means as far as grouping arrangements are concerned is only the start of the argument about social justice. We now have to ask whether there are any relevant differences that might justify deviation from the datum. Note that what has to be demonstrated is not only that certain differences justify differences of treatment, since many differences of treatment can be given *within* a mixed ability group, especially where individualised learning and teaching is the dominant method. What has to be shown is that the differences necessitate some form of grouping different from that of mixed ability.

We must start by noting that there are some differences at least that *do* warrant differential grouping. A clear example of this would be children who are wholly deaf. Such children require special skills in teaching which could not without gross waste be generalised across all teachers of mixed ability groups on the chance that a deaf child might turn up in any group. The point here is that the deaf child would *not* receive sameness of treatment if put in an ordinary mixed ability group. It is not a case of positive discrimination in the ordinary sense of that phrase, but rather a case where sameness of treatment, basic social justice, can only be approached by the recognition that this gross difference of functioning necessitates specially differentiated teaching that can only be provided in special groups. The sameness of treatment principle, therefore, is respected rather than diminished by departing from the normal datum, and it is this that requires demonstration in any claim for departure from the datum.

The same kind of claim as for the deaf child might be made for children who are simply very difficult to teach or, to put it the other way round, children with severe learning difficulties. These difficulties might variously be classified as to their causes, but this is not really to the present point. The issue would hinge essentially on the degree of special teaching skill, knowledge, or expertise needed to teach such children. If the teaching skill required is so great or so specialised that the teacher of an ordinary mixed ability group is unlikely to have it, then such a child, placed in an ordinary mixed ability group, will simply not learn at all, and in such a case the principle of sameness of treatment is only to be met by differential provision and treatment in separate groups.

Now this, of course, is an important example, since it looks like the case for accepting differences in ability as constituting relevant differences justifying departure from the datum and the arranging of education based on groups containing ability similarities. In other words, it looks like making a case for setting, rather than for mixed ability grouping. We should not rush to accept this, however. It is true that quantitative variations in the ability to learn can reach a point where a qualitative change in the teaching skill required is reached, as we have suggested above. But this does not alter the fact that across a wide range of ability ordinarily expected teaching skills should be sufficient to cope with the teaching required. Where this is the case, then to group in terms of ability similarities would sacrifice the demonstration of equal valuing for no good reason and therefore diminish the principle of sameness of treatment. Deviations from the mixed ability datum are only justified, it must be stressed, when *not* to deviate means that some pupils do not get equal valuing in terms of educational treatment if they remain in mixed ability groups.

What we have tried to demonstrate in this chapter is that mixed ability grouping, defined as grouping where each pupil is in a group as mixed in terms of abilities as any other group that he/she could be in, in a peculiar way does not require justifying because it constitutes the datum 'equality of valuing' grouping that rational agents might reasonably expect who did not yet know what their individual differences might turn out to be. Such equal valuing is to be presupposed because all persons, whatever their differences, are agents with purposes requiring the primary means to pursue them, and should demonstrably be valued as such. What requires justifying, then, and can in some cases be justified, is deviation from the datum mixed ability grouping. Such justification is achieved by demonstrating that pupils with certain specific characteristics cannot possibly receive equal valuing as purposive agents within the basic mixed ability group, or that certain activities cannot take place in mixed ability groups because of the particular demands of the activity without patently devaluing the pupils in the groups; and it is attempts at such demonstrations that should inform school discussions about whether or not to group according to ability in specific cases.

The practice of setting, as distinct from streaming, rests, of course, on claims about differences between subjects as well as differences between pupils, and this raises the question as to whether differences in the content or methodology of different teaching subjects are relevant differences for departure from the norm of mixed ability grouping. We discuss these questions in Chapter 5, but before doing so we shall look at possible connections between mixed ability teaching and the idea of fraternity.

4

Fraternity

In section 4 of Chapter 2 we noted a wide range of ideas connected with a broad notion of fraternity which often appeared in the rhetoric, and indeed sometimes the argument, supporting mixed ability grouping. We suggested there that this cluster of ideas, though often conflated with ideas of equality and social justice, was actually about something else more to do with a positive valuing of social integration and feelings of community as things to be approved of in their own right. Thus, as we pointed out, segregation of pupils into groups based upon specific abilities was seen by some teachers as deplorable, not solely because such differentiation represented the injustice of unjustifiably different treatment, but simply because it acted to support social divisiveness and against the possibility of social cohesiveness and mutually supportive co-operation. Sometimes this idea is part of a wider socio-political spectrum in which present-day society is seen as damagingly competitive, divisive and alienating, and educational arrangements of a comprehensive school and mixed ability grouping kind are seen as means of combating this state of affairs. The quotations from Crosland given in Chapter 2 appear to embrace this range of considerations. Here was at least one protagonist plainly concerned to break down divisions between schools, and within them, with the avowed object of breaking down the divisions of social class in the wider society. Social philosophers, too, have valued the idea of fraternity. We noted in the last chapter, when discussing John Rawls's criticism of the idea of equality of opportunity, that

38

such an idea was indeed to be criticised precisely because it acted against the idea of fraternity by making a fraternal society more difficult to achieve.

There thus seems to be a kind of interplay, over a range of ideas and principles, between equality and social justice on the one hand and fraternity on the other, and it is quite clear that some supporters of mixed ability grouping and other non-selective arrangements attach great importance to the fraternity end of this complex of ideas. In order to make a clear justificatory argument connected with social justice, it was necessary to separate out principles of justice from ideas of fraternity more sharply than they often are in arguments about mixed ability grouping, and it will be necessary now to do the same in considering the force of arguments based on fraternity. We shall thus operate with a notion of fraternity perhaps somewhat narrower than the richness of considerations included under that heading earlier, in order to sharpen the argument. This in no way denies the complexity of ideas intuitively motivating teachers to support one educational arrangement rather than another, but it does indicate the necessity of trying to locate logical justification with some precision.

Fraternity, of course, was one aspect of the great trinity slogan of the French Revolution: Liberty, Equality and Fraternity; but while the first two of these are still much discussed, the third has not in recent times received a great deal of attention in the literature of social justice. Indeed, inspection of the literature reveals some confusion on what the word is supposed to pick out. Although sometimes spoken of as a principle, the difficulty seems to be that fraternity really appears to indicate something about *feeling*. Liberty and equality are ways of talking about social rights and duties, but fraternity cannot be described in quite this way. It seems odd to talk about a duty to be fraternal or a right to be treated fraternally. We might applaud widespread feelings of fraternity in a society or deplore the lack of such feelings. We might, as does Bruce Ackerman in *Social Justice in the Liberal State* (1980), claim that fraternity can be overvalued in the liberal state which should go rather for liberty, equality and *individuality*. What we cannot do is command feelings of fraternity any more than we can command feelings of love and friendship. To talk therefore of a *principle* of fraternity seems inappropriate since fraternity cannot be imperative in the way a principle has to be.

The particular feelings that the term 'fraternity' picks out are clear enough. They are feelings of warmth, respect, affection and sympathy mutually felt by some persons for one another. The paradigm location for such feelings, and the true origin of the word, is in the family where it is supposed (not always correctly) that members of the family will have such feelings towards each other *for no other reason* than that they are members of the same family. The Christian idea of the brotherhood of man has the same etymological derivation, though here the denotation has clearly become extended. Thus the idea of fraternity picks out certain feelings attached to the idea of belonging, together with some positive valuation of such feelings.

Now it is probably quite true that people have such feelings and that such feelings give pleasure and satisfaction. Similarly, it is also probably true that a lack of such feelings, or the lack of an appropriate object for such feelings, is a source of discomfort. That fraternity has become considered as a good thing in its own right probably has much to do with the straightforward pleasurableness of feelings of fraternity when focused into a reciprocating group as contrasted with the discomfort of lacking such a focus or such reciprocation.

It is at this point that what we have so far discussed in terms of empirically observed feelings becomes tied up with considerations of social justice. If we start by taking fraternity as a good in some unqualified sense, then we can look for aspects of society likely to enhance or diminish opportunities for such fraternity. This is an important element in Marxism, for example. One of the criticisms of capitalist society made in important elements of Marxist thought is the alienating effect of a society in which the exploitation of one class by another, and individual isolation and competition, are encouraged by the very structure of that society. A strong emotional motivation in communist thought and action is the desire for a society in which shared ownership has removed causes for conflict and competition and replaced these disharmonies by what Plamenatz calls 'closer ties of affection and goodwill' (1975, ch. XIII, p. 380). Again, an important strand in some Christian thought is to deplore the breakdown in widespread religious conviction at least in part because this removes an appropriate focus for man's feelings of brotherhood. The difficulty of following these lines of thought is simply that some points of focus for fraternal feelings have been a great deal less universal than the brotherhood of man. The force of nationalism, for example, gathers feelings of fraternity on one location only, all too often, to use such feelings destructively against other groupings outside the favoured group. Feelings of fraternity based on race, or on social class, can similarly engender hostility against those of other races or classes.

Not only is this the case, but some ways in which feelings of fraternity can be directed actually distort our conceptions of freedom and justice. For example, as R. S. Peters points out in a relatively neglected section of his *Ethics and Education* (1966), an excessive focus of fraternal feelings on to the national state can lead to an individual's freedom being interpreted as service to the state; and justice or fairness can become interpreted as what best helps the state, or the political party, or the social class, or whatever the narrow focus of fraternity comes to be. Fraternity, in short, is not always good in itself, or necessarily productive of good instrumentally.

If this is so, then we cannot really start by assuming fraternity to be good whatever its focus and however arrived at. What we must do is to ask questions about the *appropriate* focus of fraternal feelings. To avoid inappropriate direction of fraternal feelings, and to lessen the chances of what Peters calls these 'far-fetched and fanciful transmogrifications' of fundamental principles, what should be the appropriate focus of feelings of fraternity for the rational man? Peters, as might be expected by those who know his work, is quite clear about this (p. 225):

It follows from this that there is one sort of kinship that must be appropriate for a rational being, whatever he feels about his loyalty to family, state, class, or club, and that is his kinship with other rational beings as persons. In so far as he is a rational being, and joins with other

41

rational beings in seeking to discover what ought to be done, his kinship to them as persons, with points of view to be considered, claims to be assessed impartially, and interests to pursue without unjustified interference must be considered important; for this minimal type of kinship is a precondition of the situation of practical reason. The feeling of fraternity must therefore at least be attached to the kinship of being a person.

Peters is quick to point out, however, that this ideal and justifiable focus of fraternal feelings is a long way from the actual play of such feelings in concrete communities (p. 226):

> Indeed to confront another simply as a person is to conceive of him as detached from his status and roles and from his natural affinities and associations.

This is, of course, true; but the danger does not lie so much in the unlikely occurrence of people coming to see one another simply as persons, but rather in the much more likely possibility that because of a too narrow focus of fraternal feelings they come to see others outside the focus groups of family, class, party, or state as somehow *less* than persons. The strong feelings engendered by the 'concrete communities' and their attendant loyalties actually act against the more universal feeling of kinship for all rational beings that is 'a precondition of the situation of practical reason'. In school pupils already have strong loyalties to at least some concrete communities. What they more often lack is the more generalised respect for persons as such and fraternal feelings to accompany such universal respect.

Viewed this way we have a more coherent account of the connection between the idea of fraternity and other principles of social justice and morality. In particular, and to return to the main arguments of this book, we can begin to see that the intuitive feeling some people have about selective educational arrangements being unwarrantably divisive picks out something rather more than just a plausible idea. The way in which this intuitive idea might be developed can now be explored.

We start from the idea, developed in Chapter 3, that each

person is to be equally valued, not because all are equal in all or particular respects, but because all are at least purposive agents. Valuation of particular attributes, abilities, or skills should not be pressed, in education at least, to the point where educational arrangements for these particular attributes start to act against the demonstrable valuing of each person as a purposive agent. To this can now be added the idea that the most desirable focus for fraternal feelings is upon other persons as purposive agents, and that some educational arrangements of a selective kind would tend to misdirect or wrongly focus fraternal feelings upon particular attributes, in something like the destructive way already described when such feelings are focused upon nation, social class, or political party. The idea is that although people might be valued *instrumentally* for particular purposes because they are good at mathematics, good linguists, quick thinkers, or whatever, they should only be valued *intrinsically* as persons – purposive agents – and grouping should basically be mixed ability to make this equal valuing demonstrable. Additionally, mixed ability groups would at least not act against an appropriate or justifiable focus of fraternal feelings towards fellow pupils as persons rather than as mathematicians, linguists, quick thinkers, or whatever.

To put this argument in its negative form: to set by ability of any specific kind, or to stream by some judgement of general ability, is to set up a structure where what seem to be valued are the particular or general abilities on which the setting or streaming are based. Thus the pupils suffer by being unable to perceive any valuing of themselves purely as persons, especially if in the lower sets or streams; and are also diverted from an appropriate and justifiable focus of fraternal feelings towards others purely as persons into a focus of such feelings towards those who share the presence or lack of particular or general characteristics that appear to be valued by those in authority.

When talking about pupil perceptions of their own status and value we are not, of course, talking about logical necessities but only about reasonable suppositions. But to say that the suppositions *are* reasonable is to say a lot. To be very specific: if a girl is mainly in low sets in a setting system it is difficult to

43

see how she can feel other than devalued; but even for those in high sets it is also difficult to see why they should feel valued *as persons*, for what is being valued is their skill at French, physics, or whatever. Similarly, it is difficult to see how feelings of fellowship can be directed to others as persons if the basis of daily contiguity is to be more or less specific skills and abilities.

Another way of putting all of this, and to refer back to our brief introduction to the idea of fraternity in section 4 of Chapter 2, is to say that there are indeed good grounds for favouring positive feelings towards social integration, social cohesion, a sense of community and mutual understanding and respect *provided always* that the society and community referred to is the general society and community of persons, and the mutuality to be fostered is that between persons generally. There is also good reason to suppose that such positive feelings will be best developed, or at the worst least hindered, in mixed ability groups.

It might be argued, as against all this, that the groups in which children receive instruction in schools are not the only social features of their lives. This is, of course, true; but it does not follow that all the other groups that children find themselves in are likely to encourage the universal valuing and fellowship that we have been talking about. For most of us the wrench from egocentricity, and from what Fromm called 'the incestuous ties of clan and soil' (1956, p. 69), has to be an educational development. Surely the faith of liberal education drives in this direction: that in sociality as in the development of intellect the wider and more liberating perspective will take the place of the more narrow and the more binding. Such a widening of perspective is to be facilitated and not hindered, and the more particularities of personality that children are driven to share and find their loyalties and attachments in, the less is the facilitation and the greater the hindrance.

Two further points need to be made. First, such arguments as we have used in this chapter, like those in the previous chapter, do not provide a case for making *all* groupings in a school mixed ability. What they point to is the desirability of having a basic presupposition of mixed ability grouping, divergence from which needs arguing. We have already tried to show that in some cases equal valuing of particular children can only be demonstrated by placing them in particular groups with teachers possessing peculiar skills, and further arguments for exceptions will be attempted in the next chapter. Secondly, however, although it is as true of the fraternity argument as of the equal valuing argument that it is not absolute, that exceptions might be made, it is not quite so easy to find them on the basis of the fraternity argument. Teachers often do try to engender feelings of loyalty and affection – fraternal feelings –towards teams, classes, houses, year-groups, subject groups, particular schools, and so on. Sometimes they succeed and often they fail, but in either case the justification for trying in the first place is rather dubious. The tacit understanding seems to be that to encourage such feelings towards a small group, like a team, somehow sows the seeds of the more desirable fraternity towards all persons as persons. The logic of this is doubtful since all these small-scale loyalties focus friendship within and, all too often, a concomitant enmity without. It thus does become a matter of some importance on what children are encouraged and enabled to focus fraternal feeling. In the small compass of the school, as on the greater canvas of history and politics, some foci of affections do more harm than good; and who would be bold enough to be sure that the two are not connected? It may not be the winning of battles so much as the starting of them that has its roots in the particularised loyalties of playing fields and the like.

5

Grouping, Teaching Styles and Subjects

In a recent discussion of mixed ability work in comprehensive schools a working party of Her Majesty's Inspectors noted two assumptions underlying policy decisions to adopt mixed ability grouping for all or most subjects for the first three years. One assumption concerned expectations about the skills of teachers and the other was to do with the nature of school subjects (Department of Education and Science, 1978).

The assumption about the skills of teachers was that they could competently teach not merely all levels of ability, but all levels of ability together. Special skills were usually thought necessary, noted the HMIs, only for teaching the very least able who had marked learning difficulties. If we add to this the necessity for special skills and training required to teach other special categories like the deaf, the blind and various levels of physical, mental and emotional handicap, then the assumption noted here accords with the conclusions of the last two chapters. On our argument, and for the reasons of justice, equality and fraternity given, normal teacher training should equip teachers to teach mixed ability groups.

The assumption about the nature of school subjects was that all or most subjects on the curriculum can effectively be taught in mixed ability groups, and this, say the HMIs, 'amounts to an assumption that all types of learning are equally well accomplished in one form of organisation, despite differences in the nature of the objectives, the resources used, the charac-

46

teristic activities undertaken and the kind of sequencing of learning required'. The HMIs clearly question this assumption, and, provided they recognise that it is an assumption also made by defenders of setting for all or nearly all subjects, they do well to question it. They echo arguments put forward by teachers in schools where not all subjects are taught in mixed ability groups, who defend their subjects from mixed ability grouping, and even from banding, on the ground that there is something special about the subject which makes it unsuitable for teaching in mixed ability groups.

We acknowledged in the two previous chapters that there might indeed be reasons why some kinds of teaching might be excepted from the general case in support of mixed ability grouping arising from considerations of social justice and fraternity. It might be the case that considerations about the nature of subjects could provide such excepting arguments. Such an argument would have to be strong, however, since it would need to demonstrate either that teaching subject X in a mixed ability group was logically contradictory to the nature of the subject, or that the practical difficulties in the way of success were markedly greater than those acting against success in the teaching of sets or other allegedly homogeneous groups. Only in this way could it be shown that a pupil would inevitably suffer in respect of subject X if taught in a mixed ability group, and would therefore not be valued as a learner if placed in such a group.

Three points that appear to us to be undeniable need to be made before taking up the claim for specific subject exception in more detail. First, although mixed ability groups certainly present teachers with practical problems of organisation and decision-making, it must not be thought that class teaching of setted or streamed groups is without its own problems. The connection here (that between class teaching as a method and setting or streaming as a grouping system) is not arbitrary: class teaching *does* appear to be a necessary accompaniment of setting or streaming. Unless this is the case, why is homogeneity of ability to be favoured as it is in setting or streaming? Why should homogeneity of ability be considered a virtue unless the intention is to teach pupils in some way in common? Indeed, what is often meant by saying that mixed ability groups are difficult to teach is that pupils in such groups are difficult to teach together, in common, all at the same time.

Class teaching, in its most typical form, aims at moving all pupils on together like a cohort of the old Roman Army. Indeed, it might be useful to refer to such an organisation of teaching *as* cohort teaching, where this is defined as teaching designed so as to move a whole group of pupils (considered to be similar in some respects) on from one thing to another at the same time. What the 'thing' is will of course vary: it might be a mathematical process, a scientific demonstration, an aesthetic experience, an attempt at a certain kind of expressive writing, a particular exposure to historical narrative, or whatever – but the whole group has the explanation, the practice, the experience, and so on, and then everyone moves on to another explanation, further practices, other experiences, and so on.

Now the difficulties here are many. Most of them centre on the difficulty of organising and presenting explanations, practices and activities in such a way that all pupils will accept, understand and respond within the same space of time and with a reasonably similar output of work and a similarly timed readiness to move on to the next part of the teacher's plan. There are two direct consequences of the attempt to reach this ideal: some pupils are bored and some pupils fail. The bored, of course, are those who would have been ready to move on with less explanation and less practice than they have had to receive – ironically they are often given more practice because they finish the set amount quickly! – and the failures are those who never understand or complete in the time given. Somewhere in the middle, perhaps, is the pupil for whom the particular piece of teaching was ideal. Setting and streaming, of course, aims at minimising this difficulty, but since ability ranges are continua and not discrete steps, the difficulty always remains.

Class teaching, then, is neither obviously successful nor without difficulties, and any difficulties of teaching mixed ability groups by other techniques must be judged against these.

Our second and connected point is that empirical evidence

clearly demonstrates a vast and complex range of individual differences among pupils. We have known for a very long time that across a very wide range of characteristics affecting learning pupils differ markedly one from another, that many of these characteristics are specific and unrelated, and that dynamic change in these characteristics also varies from individual to individual. It is the very existence of these differences that is sometimes advanced in support of setting or streaming, but in fact the outcome of their existence and their complexity is that no allegedly homogeneous group can actually *be* homogeneous in all respects affecting learning within the group. Individuals will differ in their ability to listen, concentrate and understand; they will vary as to their critical thinking, their sensitivity to criticism, their acuity of perception, their thresholds of anxiety and their tolerance of the tedious; they will differ as to their interests, their pleasures, their capacity to discriminate and to reason. No catch-all concept like 'ability' or 'intelligence' can possibly hold all this without spillage. No group, however setted or streamed, can be without significant variety.

The third of our points closely relates to the two already made. It is that understanding is only meaningful in the educational context when it refers to what goes on in an individual mind. Of course, interaction between individuals can assist understanding, and it could certainly be well argued that such social exchange is necessary for any relatively sophisticated understanding to develop at all. But this social exchange, however important, is only facilitative of understanding, and not what the understanding actually is. To put this more directly: if all but Freddy in Mr Baker's class have understood the mechanism of photosynthesis, Mr Baker may be tempted to say that his class has understood. This is wrong, not only because Mr Baker has failed to take account of Freddy, but because there is no sense in which a *class* can be said to have understood other than as a shorthand for Bob understands, Jane understands, Mary understands, and so on. This is not the trivial point it might seem, however obvious it is once stated. It is an important point because, in what we have called cohort teaching, there is always the assumption that each pupil will reach his or her own understanding at the same time. This is a necessary assumption since the cohort must make the next cognitive advance together; but it is an assumption that is rarely satisfied in practice where, as we have already noted, the teacher all too often must judge between boring some individuals with unnecessary repetition or, more often, accepting that some individuals have not properly understood.

With these three points in mind – the sometimes unremarked difficulties attaching to class teaching, the inescapable and wide variety of individual differences, and the necessity of understanding taking place in individual minds – we can now look more closely at the varied nature of different subjects and the way this might affect claims for exception from the norm of mixed ability grouping.

Let us consider first the response made by some mathematics teachers when asked in the NFER inquiry whether they considered their subject suitable for mixed ability teaching:

> Approximately half of those interviewed considered [mathematics] totally unsuitable for mixed ability teaching largely because they perceived it as having a logical structure through which pupils must proceed in a prescribed way ... Frequent comments pertaining to the 'laddered', 'structured', 'sequential', 'linear' and 'cumulative' qualities of mathematics indicated the nature of perceptions held by a majority of teachers in the sample. (Reid *et al.*, 1981, p. 130)

Now if the nature of mathematics is correctly perceived here, and we shall accept that it is for the present, all it demonstrates is that *each individual mind* must advance in understanding through the necessary structure. It says nothing at all about any necessity for thirty or so pupils to advance in a 'linear' or 'laddered' way *all at the same time*. Indeed, it is easily seen that to attempt to make all thirty advance at the same time, to make the same progress, is the most likely way of ensuring strain and failure for some. What really follows from this perception of the nature of mathematics is not the cohort teaching that the teachers seem to suppose, but a teaching technique that will facilitate individual learning. Yet, although individual teaching techniques were used frequently by twenty-one out of forty-three teachers of mathematics in the inquiry, they were only dominant in the methods of three teachers.

The general point to emerge from this brief consideration of mathematics teaching really applies to any subject area where the understanding and skills to be developed are essentially of an intellectual and individual kind. Many school subjects are like this: science subjects, mathematics, language learning, economics, geography, history, for example, all involve non-arbitrary frameworks of concepts and propositions which have to be grasped in particular sequences and/or patterns by individual minds. What is true about all of these subjects, and others more or less like them, is that since the important structures of understanding *are* non-arbitrary they have to be understood in some sense in the same way. Coefficients of expansion, quadratic equations, regular verbs, supply and demand curves, river formation and the consequences of wars are not the kinds of 'goings on' that can be understood in any old way: they have criteria of correctness. Indeed, and interestingly, the tighter the criteria of correctness seem to be, the more status the subjects appear to have, and the more generally such subjects are defended against mixed ability grouping, as the NFER inquiry shows. But, as with the mathematics example, the point about the non-arbitrariness of the understanding to be achieved, undoubtedly correct, is *not* the most important point when considering whether to arrange pupils for the teaching of these subjects in mixed ability groups or not. The important and relevant point is that the structured understanding must take place in individual minds *and* that the pace at which such understanding develops is almost certain to vary between individuals in *any* group, however it is organised.

If this reasoning is sound, it means that teaching approaches to the kinds of subjects being considered here, those depending upon correctly structured and sequenced individual understandings, should largely be individualised. That is, teaching should be so arranged as to facilitate varying individual rates of learning and understanding. If this is so, then the main argument for defending these subjects from mixed

51

ability grouping disappears, for the slight convenience to the teacher of doing her individualised teaching to a group of roughly similar abilities is not a sufficient counter to the arguments of justice and fraternity in favour of mixed ability grouping outlined in Chapters 3 and 4. There is, at the very least, no logical necessity for these subjects to be taught in classes that are setted, banded, or streamed.

Before looking at some subjects that do, perhaps, come closer to demonstrating features that require more homogeneous ability groups for teaching, there are some general remarks that need to be made about individualised learning arrangements. Such arrangements are often attacked by criticising features that are not essential to such arrangements. For example, it is no necessary feature of individualised learning arrangements that pupils work in isolation, having no communication one with another. In fact, it is often more characteristic of such arrangements that children are encouraged to seek help from one another as well as from a teacher. Neither is it the case that a teacher is barred, as it were, from teaching a group of pupils or discussing something with a group of pupils where this becomes necessary and possible because of the stage the pupils have reached. Such groupings, however, would be opportunist and temporary conveniences rather than permanent arrangements.

Another feature often attacked, for example by HMI's writing about mixed ability geography teaching (Department of Education and Science, 1978, p. 103), is the use of individual work sheets 'preceded by a precis of information supplied by the teacher'. Work sheets, or some ways of indicating individual assignments, do seem to be necessary in some form for individual work. Clearly, like blackboard work, OHP transparencies, or duplicated material used in class teaching, such work sheets or assignment materials can be good or bad in design and production; at least they do, or should, allow for variations in reading ability and other factors affecting learning, and we can see no reason whatsoever for attributing any essential or universal harmfulness to such materials. In the geographical example noted, it appears to be the precis of information supplied by the teacher that draws the critical fire. It is alleged that 'Pupils are thereby deprived of the opportunity of consulting a range of sources, of assessing one point of view against another, or of making a choice of what they perceive to be relevant and significant' (p. 103). But, again, why should this *necessarily* be so? Surely it all depends on what the teacher's precis actually says, and on what the pupils are asked to do. If *any* duplicated material given to pupils, in a mixed ability *or* a class teaching context, has this effect, then of course it is harmful; but this is true of all teaching arrangements, not only in individualised learning ones. Arguments directed against mixed ability grouping, individualised learning arrangements, or any other educational prescriptions must focus on the *necessary features* of such prescriptions if they are to be successfully countervailing.

Practical difficulties of organising, directing and managing individualised learning in mixed ability groups is considerable, and comments directed to this have some point. These doubts only take on an Aunt Sally character when it is supposed, as it often is, that it is *only* individualised learning that presents difficulties. Teaching mixed ability groups by class teaching methods presents even greater difficulties, and yet is quite common; and as already mentioned, the successes claimed with class teaching methods in allegedly homogeneous groups in sets or streams are usually unjustified. That the practical difficulties of individualised learning and teaching can be overcome is indicated by the growing literature in which teachers report their experiences in this work (*Cambridge Journal of Education*, 1976; Sewell, 1980).

There is another group of subjects, not usually thought of as 'intellectual', but where the skills to be developed are similarly individual. What is markedly different about this group of subjects is that teachers of them have long been used to teaching them in mixed ability groups in a relatively individualised way. We refer here to those subjects in which the pupil is required to develop individual practical skills. Such subjects include practical art, craft subjects like needlework, woodwork and metalwork, some approaches to design and technology which emphasise individual making, and office skills like typing. So far as we can see teachers of these subjects have always recognised that pupils progress in their acquisition of the skills at individually different rates. A normal lesson in these areas reveals pupils working at different things at different speeds with the teacher helping and teaching individually. On the whole it does not seem to matter if the groups taking these subjects are *deemed* to be mixed ability or not, as their teachers have always accepted them as being of mixed ability *in the relevant aptitudes, skills and information*, even if allegedly homogeneous in whatever measure of ability the school uses for its grouping. It is interesting to reflect, however, why differential abilities are more obvious in the teaching and learning of specific practical skills than in those areas, previously mentioned, where the intellectual understandings to be developed are no less individual. Could it be that the material objects being produced in most of the craft-type activities reveal very obviously the differential progress and the folly of supposing that pupils can start and finish everything at the same time? Could it be that materials must not be wasted and therefore projects *must* be brought to a finish? Would it were the case that the waste and distortion of minds, the incompleted conceptual framework, the as-yet-ungrasped logical relationship frequently occurring in the class teaching of the intellectual subjects could be similarly obvious, standing about the room for all to see!

We come now to some activities and learnings distinguished from others by the fact that they *necessarily* involve pupils with groups in the sense that the activity just cannot take place at all unless pupils interact with one another. For example, while it is not at all odd to imagine a person learning and practising mathematics on his own, or on his own with a teacher, learning and practising football or discussion on one's own seems odd at least and is probably impossible. Where the activity necessarily involves a group, and individualised learning would be a nonsense, then the constitution of the group, that is, its homogeneity or heterogeneity as to the abilities, skills and information possessed by individuals within it, becomes a highly relevant consideration linked with teaching and learning requirements. The point here is that if we were to insist dogmatically that groups for the teaching of subjects necessarily requiring groups were to be of mixed ability, we might find that some pupils could not learn at all in such a setting. This would go against our principle of equal valuing, since you do

[margin note: hetrogeneity; diverse; composed of diverse elements. homogeneity; of the same kind of nature; uniform.]

not demonstrate your equal valuing of a person by placing her in a situation where she cannot learn. We need to be sure of our ground here because the kinds of subject we are now talking about are often considered by teachers to be quite suitable for mixed ability grouping. In the NFER study no teachers, for example, thought integrated humanities studies unsuitable for mixed ability teaching, yet this is an area where discussion is extensively used; and only some 11 per cent of teachers thought physical education unsuitable for mixed ability teaching even though, presumably, this includes team games. It is at least possible to argue that the rationales of these teachers have not been thought through clearly.

Examples of the kind of learning that necessarily involves discussion are to be found in much of the study associated with the humanities and the social sciences. If we take the view of the Schools Council Humanities Curriculum Project, then discussion is certainly a necessary technique in these areas of the curriculum. But we do not need to go as far as this in order to suggest that an exchange of views, perspectives and understandings, going beyond those of the teacher, ought properly to be part of the learning experience of any pupil being introduced to the humanities or the social sciences. If we accept this, and if we want the discussion to be beneficial, then perhaps there would have to be some limit upon the differential mix within the group engaged in discussion. Beyond a certain point of differential ability or information the exchange of talk within the group ceases to be a discussion. People freely seeking others to engage in discussion normally seek those of at least relatively equal ability and information. That they are reasonable in doing so may well follow from the nature of discussion, so that we are making, as it were, a conceptual point. But anyone who has tried to get discussion going in school with a group of markedly diverse ability or information will be well aware of the practical nature of this difficulty. Groups formed primarily for discussion, it may be argued then, should be relatively homogeneous as to the ability and information possessed by the members, and this conclusion *is* to do with the nature and logic of the activity.

There are other activities, necessarily taking place in groups, where it could be argued that similar considerations apply. Consider team games like football and hockey, the playing of music in small or large ensembles, and dramatic activities. In all these cases, and others like them, those freely seeking association in these activities seek out relative equals to play with and to act with and, in the case of team games, to play against. It may be that this is more of a logical matter than is sometimes supposed, but there is no need to press this point. Even if the matter is contingent it remains observable that there are satisfactions in all these activities only properly to be gained with those persons relatively equal to oneself in the relevant skills and information. Correspondingly, there are satisfactions to be thwarted and frustrated if the ability and information mix is too diverse. The teaching and organisational problems of the teacher increase, and the likelihood of each pupil learning successfully diminishes proportionately to the degree of mix. Thus, again, it can be argued that to insist dogmatically on these activities taking place in mixed ability groups actually acts against the principle of equal valuing, since at least some pupils, and probably considerable numbers, would be deprived of proper opportunities for learning.

This conclusion is strangely against the fashion, as briefly noted above. It is often in these particular activities that mixed ability grouping is advocated, either on the ground that it does not matter if they are mixed or, more strongly, that it is of positive advantage so to mix. The 'does not matter' attitude is worthy of note, since we might argue that what is going on here is more to do with the status than with the nature of the subject. The assumption often seems to be that for low-status subjects it does not matter if they take place in mixed ability groups, whereas for high-status subjects it does. Games, music, humanities subjects, discussion and drama are not considered high-status subjects by some people, and therefore are considered suitable for mixed ability grouping if mixed ability grouping there must be. This only makes sense on some covert assumption that mixed ability grouping is harmful and that we only need to worry about protecting the important from harm! As against this it can be suggested that where mixed ability grouping might be harmful – that is, prevent pupils from learning properly and therefore not value

56

them – is precisely in these areas where pupils need to work together in groups because of the nature of the subject. These are the activities that, at least arguably, need homogeneous groups to some extent. It is perhaps worth emphasising that the abilities, skills and information in which the group is held to be homogeneous must be relevant to the activity being engaged in. For example, in respect of football, the point is not that all the pupils in a group should be similar in respect of IQ scores or reading ability, only that they should have roughly equivalent football skills and information.

There is a rather different argument to be noted which presents collaborative work by children in mixed ability groups as the paradigm form of mixed ability teaching. On this view mixed ability groups for discussion, drama and games are to be favoured because they provide exactly the opportunities for children to learn, first, that all children can make some kind of useful contribution to a group activity and, secondly, how to work so as to enable each of the group's members to contribute something worthwhile. This extract from E. M. Hoyles' account of mixed ability teaching at Vauxhall Manor school reflects this kind of view (1975, p.61):

One of the main features of mixed ability classroom organisation is the numerous occasions on which children need to work in groups. The child has to learn how to use the group activity effectively from the beginning. First of all, she needs to learn how to play her own part in the group... In addition, she will need to grow in judgement of other people's ability and this can join the general teaching the school provides in respect for other people because, from an early stage, she will have to learn how to use other people's talents, not only for her own development but for the development of the group. It is important for her to learn how to apportion work to other members of the group so that when she becomes a leader she can use other people's talents to the full. In addition, there is a great need for learning tolerance since it will be impossible for every member of the

57

group to fulfil exactly what the group expects and therefore, she will need to understand not only the abilities of others but also their failings and how they can best be helped.

Teachers involved in the Cambridge DES Regional Course action research on mixed ability teaching suggested similarly that 'Excessive use of individual learning techniques, e.g. work cards, might be in danger of preventing social benefits arising from mixed ability grouping' (Elliott *et al.*, 1978, p. 7). On this account it is thus group work itself, rather than individualised learning, that is seen by some at least as the paradigm of mixed ability teaching.

The roots of this argument, like those of the argument already presented, are in the principles of equality and fraternity. What is stressed in this account, however, is not just the equal value of each child as a learner, but his or her equal potential value as a *source* of learning, as a *contributor* to group activity and, perhaps by extension, to society at large. Since this is clearly a position of uncertain empirical standing, it may be presented alternatively as an advocacy of the desirability of treating people *as if* they all had a worthwhile contribution to make. An argument in support of this act of faith is largely on the grounds of the power of such a conviction, or its negation, to become self-fulfilling (cf. the argument cited previously about labelling children). It arises out of a desire to extend the equal value principle beyond a perhaps rather grudging concession that all people share, however minimally, in some basic and common human attributes, to a more whole-hearted embracing of them as beings who can, if we enable them to do so, contribute positively to our society and to our lives.

What perhaps is crucial to the question at issue here is the extent to which all members of a mixed ability group can in fact contribute, or can be enabled to contribute, to learning in a given field or style of activity. As the members of the Nottingham Teacher Education Project properly observed: 'Group work and oral work may either help the less able, or discourage them, depending on how they are organised' (Dooley *et al.*, 1977, p. 8). If, given the right support and encouragement, all members of a group can contribute usefully to a discussion or a game, then the demands of both our lines of argument are satisfied and the case in favour of mixed ability grouping for these subjects is made. If they *really* cannot, then the second argument, in favour of relatively homogeneous groups for these subjects, succeeds. The caution, which we should take seriously however, is not to dismiss the potential contribution which might be made to collaborative group work by 'the less able' before we have explored imaginatively the range of conditions which enable such a contribution to be made.

In this chapter we have looked for arguments supporting the exception of subjects from the normal datum of mixed ability grouping and we have differed in some of our conclusions from those often advanced. We have argued that since 'intellectual' subjects, typified by mathematics and science, seek to produce understanding in individual minds and are not *essentially* group activities, they should be taught by methods which recognise the diversity of rates of individual understanding; and that the perhaps marginally greater difficulty of doing this in mixed ability groups does not constitute a strong enough argument to countervail the case for mixed ability grouping in terms of equal valuing and fraternity. The same argument, we have said, applies to subjects of an art and craft kind, where the skills to be acquired are largely practical but nevertheless still essentially individual; though we have noted here that teachers of these skills and arts have long operated with groups that are mixed as to the relevant abilities anyway. On the other hand, it has been suggested that there are some activities that are group activities of necessity, and in these cases the relative homogeneity of the group in respect of *relevant* abilities and information does seem desirable, since without it some pupils would find it difficult to acquire the appropriate skills, attitudes, or knowledge, and deliberately to put them in such a situation would not be to demonstrate equal valuing of them.

Finally we have noted the argument which emphasises the collaborative nature of group work and the valuation of group members as contributors, and which would see the very diversity of these contributions in a mixed ability situation as a virtue.

Although these arguments do not all point in the same direction, leaving as they do room for judgement in particular cases, they do all rest on the same basic principle. Briefly stated, that principle is that the issue of whether to group on a basis of mixed ability or not is to be decided by asking what arrangement, in a particular teaching and learning activity, will most patently demonstrate the equal valuing of pupils as learners themselves and contributors to the learning of others.

6

The Lessons of Experience

In our argument so far we have tried to show some kind of logical connection between certain fundamental values and premises about human nature on the one hand and certain kinds of educational practices on the other. The precise character of the logical connections which we have drawn may deserve closer scrutiny in a more technical philosophical work than this one pretends to be. They are certainly not all of a piece. In some cases we have suggested that there might be quite a tight logical entailment, such that a commitment to principle A necessarily implied a commitment to practice X. In other cases the connection was looser – X might be one form of practice but perhaps not the only one which reflected or was consistent with the principle. Though we have from time to time referred to evidence of the actual consequences of one kind of practice or another, it has not in general depended upon such evidence. In slightly more technical terms our argument has been very largely *a priori* in character. Inevitably an argument of this kind will be an incomplete argument. There will be a number of questions of direct relevance to the issue at hand which remain unanswered. In particular, the question 'What are the *actual effects* of mixed ability grouping on children's social relations, educational careers, or classroom learning?' is not one which can be answered on the basis of *a priori* reasoning. This requires experience, observation and evidence. We can examine philosophically the reasons for seeking certain intended or hoped for effects, or the desirability or otherwise of other effects when known. We can even

61

observe logical features of practices of a kind which provide good (though perhaps not sufficient) reason to predict what their effects will be. But in the end philosophers overreach themselves if they try to prescribe educational (or any other) practices without consideration of the actual and not just the intended or anticipated outcomes of those practices. The arguments we have presented so far need, then, to be considered alongside empirical evidence available in other sources relating to the effects of different forms of grouping and different styles of group teaching.

There have, of course, been literally hundreds of studies of grouping in schools, and we cannot do full justice to them here. However, certain trends do emerge fairly clearly. These are well summarised in one of the most recent and comprehensive studies which we have already referred to several times, the NFER research conducted by Reid *et al.* (1981). The conclusion that research leads to is that 'There are no certain outcomes, either positive or negative, which can be assumed to follow inevitably from mixed ability grouping or, probably, from any other form of organisation. What is achieved or not achieved for the pupil, in academic, social and personal terms, will depend on a complex array of circumstances' (p. 157).

In an earlier paper which attempted to review research findings on teaching groups in secondary schools, Corbishley presented a similar picture. The three main conclusions which he drew are as follows (1977, pp. 2–4):

(1) 'attainment as measured by standardised tests is not directly or consistently affected by variations in grouping practices' – i.e. success depends on their combination with other variables;
(2) 'the social effects of particular grouping practices vary across time and across national boundaries' – again, other local features seem to be significant in combination with grouping practices;
(3) 'the teacher in the classroom is shown, or presented as, or inferred to be the crucial factor in determining the "success" of any form of grouping. If teachers favour streaming it works, if mixed ability, then that too works.'

Now although these kinds of research finding are sobering and though they clearly indicate that 'going mixed ability' will in itself produce no instant miracle of educational or social change, they are not entirely discouraging to the line of argument presented in this book. What the research evidence suggests is that mixed ability grouping will not be sufficient by itself to realise the sort of values we have defended. More usefully, it points to some of the other conditions which will need to be satisfied if mixed ability grouping is to have the kind of effects that are hoped for. Among those are the following.

First, the teachers responsible for mixed ability groups will need to understand and support the rationale of this form of organisation. We should hardly need research findings to tell us that innovation imposed on an uncomprehending or hostile staff stands little chance of achieving its hoped for benefits.

Secondly, the teachers responsible for mixed ability groups will need to develop teaching styles and strategies appropriate to the variety of individual attainment, motivation, and so on, in the group. Again, it will hardly be surprising if the organisational change is ineffectual unless supported by appropriate pedagogy.

Thirdly, and perhaps by extension of the first two points, to be effective the change to mixed ability teaching needs to be associated with a fairly radical change of attitude and perspective which runs through every aspect of school life. This last lesson is drawn particularly effectively in Stephen Ball's study of Beechside Comprehensive (1981). Ball tries to explain why it is that the most striking aspect of the analysis of mixed ability forms in his study is the absence of dramatic change. His message is clear (p. 286):

> Mixed ability is unlikely to involve radical changes in schooling while 'the organising notions' embodied in the teachers' attitudes and views of the classroom remain essentially unchanged. It is apparent that most of the teachers continue to behave in, and to think of, 'types' of children.

At school level, as at classroom level, the old selective processes continue to operate in spite of the pattern of mixed ability organisation, and so (p. 284):

> While school values are still essentially concerned with competition and the primacy of academic success, the mixed ability system continues to feed its pupils more or less 'efficiently' into examination courses of different status and different negotiable value further up in the school.

It is illuminating to compare these three conditions – conditions of the success of mixed ability teaching, according to the evidence – with the actual circumstances in which schools have often reorganised their grouping. The picture presented by the ILEA and HMI reports, for example, suggests that all too often the innovation has been imposed on a staff which has had precious little part in the decision, is divided on its merits and is unprepared for the new pedagogic demands whose satisfaction is crucial to its success. What we can learn from the frustrations of this experience is that the promotion of the values which some people have seen as expressed in mixed ability grouping must rely upon a deeper appreciation of its rationale and its underlying values, and a wider appreciation of those aspects of pedagogy and school organisation which may support or conflict with that rationale and the values in which it is grounded. We hope that this book may contribute to the development of this appreciation.

7

'Going Mixed Ability' – Who Should Decide?

We have presented in the preceding chapters something of a case in support of mixed ability grouping in schools. We think it is a fairly plausible case and one which rests upon rational argument rather than crude assertion, unexamined prejudice, or mistaken inference. To that extent we might expect that anyone who followed the argument carefully would be drawn to roughly the same conclusions as ourselves. Nevertheless, we have to concede that this will in practice be an unlikely outcome. The issue of mixed ability grouping is now and is likely to remain a controversial one, even among those who have examined the arguments carefully.

There may be a number of points at issue which can account for this controversy. People will assess differently the cost, in terms of manpower, time and resources, of a change in the pattern of school organisation. They will take different views of the actual effects of mixed ability grouping in particular schools (as distinct from the general effects as revealed by wide-ranging surveys). They may draw different implications from the ones we have drawn from the translation of principles or values into educational practice. They may dissent from one or other of the basic values or principles which underlie our whole argument, or at least wish to weigh in the same scales other values with contrary implications. For these and no doubt other reasons our contribution to the literature on mixed ability grouping may add fuel to the controversy but is unlikely to resolve it.

If, then, the question whether or not to have mixed ability teaching in a school is one on which there is unlikely to be a consensus either among the teaching profession or in the wider community, we are faced with the problem of how a decision on this aspect of school policy is to be arrived at, or more plainly, who should decide.

One approach to the question of who should decide rests upon an analysis of the nature of the decision to be made. This is to say, we can consider, first, what sort of a question it is, what sort of knowledge, understanding, or judgement is required to answer it, and on this basis consider who would be best equipped or qualified, who would have the relevant expertise, to answer it; who, on this criterion, should determine whether schools or a particular school should or should not 'go mixed ability' or indeed return from a mixed ability pattern of organisation to one based on streams, bands, or sets.

Examination of this question does not point clearly in one direction. Certainly some of the considerations which are relevant seem to relate to matters which one might judge to be within the special expertise of teachers or headteachers. These might include, for example, knowledge of the abilities, including the span of abilities, of children in a particular school; knowledge of the resources available within the school, including the pedagogic skills of teachers and their ability to take on different styles of teaching; understanding of the logical structure of different subjects and of styles of pedagogy appropriate to that structure (see Chapter 5 above); understanding of the actual response of a given population of children to one or more patterns of school organisation. Teachers are perhaps not always as well informed on all these matters as one might wish them to be, but nevertheless we suggest that they are generally better informed about them than most people outside schools – and this provides some basis for the claim that they (i.e. the teachers) should make decisions on such questions as the form of grouping adopted in a school.

It doesn't seem to me that streaming is the concern of groups in society other than teachers. Streaming hasn't anything to do with anything – except efficiency in teaching. (Headmaster quoted in Jackson, 1964, p. 43)

The issue is not, however, as straightforward as this Northampton headteacher would make out. For, if it has done nothing else, this book must surely have given ample illustration to the observation that questions about how to group children in schools rest upon fundamental judgements about the moral, social and political principles and values which are to be served by that grouping structure. Those arguing for or against mixed ability grouping refer with different emphasis and different enthusiasm to such principles as equality of opportunity, equality of achievement, equality of value, fraternity, individual excellence, respect for people as individuals or as persons, the intrinsic value of competitiveness, social cohesion, and so on. The argument about mixed ability grouping is, quite unavoidably, an argument rooted in judgements about the application of, and the weight to be given to, these values.

But who has special authority or expertise in judgements of this kind? Here it is much less easy to accept that teachers have special knowledge or wisdom which sets them above the general population. Indeed, it is a feature of a democratic society that it is sceptical of the claims of *any* particular sector of that society to have special expertise or authority on what is good for society as a whole. It prefers instead to allow such questions to be resolved through the emergence of some kind of consensus, through the competing demands of individual preferences, or, if the worst comes to the worst, by majority vote. These are the procedures demanded by a morally sceptical or morally pluralistic democratic society.

Our consideration of the nature of the judgement involved here does not, then, point clearly to a single category of people with exclusive qualification to pronounce on the question. It indicates rather that it is the sort of question which teachers might claim to have special but not exclusive competence to judge, the sort of question which might appropriately be determined not by teachers alone but collectively by, or on the basis of consultation between, teachers and other people in a community whose interests are affected by the decision.

We believe that we reach the same kind of conclusion if we approach the question 'Who should decide?' in a different way – if we consider, for example, the *practicality* of leaving the issue to be decided exclusively by teachers in a particular school or, more radically, by the schools, parents and/or the local community.

We have already referred to empirical evidence (see Chapter 6) which points to the unproductive consequences for a school whose teachers adopt mixed ability grouping without a fairly thoroughgoing commitment both to its principles and to its implications. Even worse is the frustration and resentment engendered where mixed ability organisation is imposed on an unwilling staff by a zealous head or by a crusading minority (though it is sometimes overlooked that teachers obliged to work in a streamed school against their better judgement may be just as frustrated and resentful). It is difficult to accept, therefore, that it would be very productive to locate the decision about school grouping entirely outside the school, even if in terms of wider political entitlement this seemed justifiable. Parents and others in the wider community require the positive co-operation of teachers, and not just their grudging acquiescence, if social values and social policies are to take life within the structure of a school.

But, equally, as one report after another has emphasised in recent years, the task which schools face is too demanding for them to undertake without the support of, let alone in the face of, opposition from parents and others in the wider community.

The Taylor Committee, for example, concluded:

To sum up, teachers need informed support. The society of which schools are a part can and does question their performance, but schools in turn need the understanding and help of society in their difficult task. Only a working partnership can meet these needs ... (Department of Education and Science, 1977, p. 52)

Teachers can expect to succeed only very rarely in promoting among children a view of themselves, attitudes towards each other and a set of social values which are constantly negated by the contrary pressures of those outside the school. Practicality therefore demands that if teachers wish to promote a particular set of values or attitudes among their pupils, and particularly perhaps if they want to change existing attitudes and values, then they will need to ally to their own efforts all the support they can get from those outside the school. But support is not support if it is not firmly grounded. Joan Sallis expresses the basic argument here and its implications in a succinct equation (1977, p. 25):

The case [for wider participation in school affairs] is essentially that the job schools now have to do cannot be done adequately without more support from parents and the community in general. Support means consent; consent means understanding; true understanding can only come from responsibility.

Once again we come to the conclusion that a policy decision about the form of grouping to be adopted in a school is one that should not be taken *exclusively* either by a school, by teachers, by the parents or community who have a stake in its affairs, or, if it comes to that, by their political representatives. It is pre-eminently the kind of issue which is properly and best resolved through a process of collaborative discussion and negotiation. 'Mixed ability teaching is an appropriate topic on which to begin dialogue between teachers and society' (Elliott, 1976, p. 13).

If this seems a modest conclusion, it nevertheless appears to represent a radical departure from recent practice. The 1981 NFER study, for example, reports that in *none* of the twenty-nine schools involved in its research had parents' views been sought concerning the grouping practices to be adopted. Indeed, in a number of cases schools seemed almost to be deliberately obscuring their policies on this issue from parental inquiry. What precisely is a parent to understand, for example, by this information from the school brochure? 'The school does not practice [sic] a rigid policy of streaming at any level except where it is appropriate.' (All classes in the first two years in this school were in fact mixed ability.) In half the schools studied by Margaret Reid and her colleagues 'there were even fewer clues as to how teaching groups were organised, the topic being either not mentioned at all or sparse and general information given' (Reid *et al.*, 1981, pp. 43–44).

Almost certainly among the motives of heads who chose to be so discreet about their grouping practices was a concern to protect what they believed to be an important progressive innovation from the ill-informed criticism of a reactionary or narrow-sighted set of parents. If we have some sympathy for their concerns we have little hope for their long-term success. Indeed, we are tempted to offer as partial explanation of both the limited achievements of progressive developments in education in the 1960s and early 1970s and the more recent wobble of confidence in the education system the failure of schools to ensure the understanding and support of parents or the wider society for the innovations upon which teachers were engaged. The reorientation of values and attitudes which is embodied in mixed ability grouping is, we believe, too radical to succeed without the understanding and support of the teachers *and* the parents of the children whose lives and educational careers they are designed to shape.

Notes on Further Reading

For the general reader there are two articles in particular which provide a useful review of the considerable quantity of empirical research on mixed ability grouping. Those are Esposito's article 'Homogeneous and heterogeneous ability groupings: principle findings and implications for evaluating and designing more effective educational environments' in the 1973 *Review of Educational Research* and, slightly more up to date, Corbishley's 1977 contribution to the collection of papers edited by Davies and Cave. These two articles give ample reference to the many more specific studies which have been conducted. The even more recent NFER study by Margaret Reid and her colleagues, *Mixed Ability Teaching: Problems and Possibilities* (1981), is a work to which we have made considerable reference in our text. It is a particularly useful source for information about how and why mixed ability grouping has been introduced in secondary schools. Its focus is on teachers' perceptions of the advantages and disadvantages of this pattern of organisation rather than on any attempt to test independently its consequences, but is no less illuminating or indeed credible for that. Stephen Ball's study of Beechside Comprehensive school (1981) provides empirical evidence of a different kind – this time based on a detailed case study of one institution. Its focus is on the problem of institutional change in a school which is attempting to 'go mixed ability'.

Two official reports provide an interesting, though not always clearly distinguished, mixture of information and comment on mixed ability grouping. These are the 1976 report by the ILEA Inspectorate, *Mixed Ability Grouping*, and the HMI report – Number 6 in the Matters for Discussion series – *Mixed Ability Work in Comprehensive Schools* (1978). The HMI report in particular raises many of the issues which we have tried to develop in this book.

Most of the works which begin to develop critical consideration of the principles underlying mixed ability grouping are collections of articles. The best of these, though it includes some pretty diverse material, is *Mixed Ability Teaching in Secondary Schools*, edited by Davies and Cave. Brian Davies's own contribution to the collection is both sane and provocative. A. V. Kelly has contributed substantially to the literature both as editor (*Case Studies in Mixed Ability Teaching*, 1975) and writer (*Mixed Ability Teaching: Theory and Practice*, 1978). His own writing is always clear and straightforward, but we have not found much in the way of original thinking in these books, which tend to stop short of the more fundamental questions. One of the most thoughtful books we found on the subject was Pat Daunt's *Comprehensive Values* (1975). This is an admirable attempt by a headmaster of substantial intellect and humane instinct to articulate a philosophy of comprehensive education. While its subject is much wider than mixed ability grouping, there is both direct reference and indirect application to this issue in much of what is written.

We have tried to relate the fundamental argument laid out in Chapters 3 and 4 to some recent writing in moral, social and political philosophy. This literature is perhaps more heavygoing than much of the literature on mixed ability grouping, but is helpful to explore it if the really important underlying issues and justifications are to be considered. Alan Gewirth's *Reason and Morality* (1978) is a good example of work in this area of philosophy, and much of our argument derives from the characteristics of freedom, knowledge and self-esteem that Gewirth deems to be necessities for any purposive agent. John Rawls's *A Theory of Justice* (1972) has already proved one of the most influential books on political philosophy in recent years and cannot really be neglected by educators wrestling with problems of distributive justice. Another work, not mentioned by us specifically in the text, but one which contributes significantly to recent philosophical discussion of liberal ideas, is Robert Nozick's *Anarchy, State and Utopia*. Bruce Ackerman's *Social Justice in the Liberal State* (1980), which has a twenty-three-page chapter on liberal education, discusses fraternity, as does Rawls; but the most perceptive treatment of fraternity is probably still to be found in Richard Peters's *Ethics and Education* (1966). Fraternity can be considered in relation to the idea of alienation much discussed by Marxist writers. A good discussion of both of these concepts and their relationship is to be found in John Plamenatz's work *Karl Marx's Philosophy of Man* (1975).

There are at least three works which provide starting-points for those thinking about mixed ability grouping from the point of view of particular subjects. Teacher opinion on this, resulting from one particular inquiry, is displayed in the 1981 NFER report by Margaret Reid and her colleagues. More positive descriptions of what some teachers do with mixed ability groups in various subject areas are to be found in the special edition of the *Cambridge Journal of Education*, vol. 6, nos 1/2 (1976), and in the interesting collection of articles on *Mixed Ability Teaching* edited by C. Sewell (1980). The value of these two sources lies especially in their demonstration by practising teachers of what can be done even in subject areas often considered difficult for mixed ability teaching.

Select Bibliography

This bibliography contains all the works directly referred to in the text along with a small number of additional references which are particularly relevant to the argument in this book.

Ackerman, B. A. (1980), *Social Justice in the Liberal State* (New Haven, Conn.: Yale University Press).

Bailey, C. H. (1976), 'Mixed ability teaching and the defence of subjects', *Cambridge Journal of Education*, vol. 6, nos 1/2, pp. 24–31.

Ball, S. J. (1981), *Beechside Comprehensive: A Case Study of Secondary Schooling* (Cambridge: Cambridge University Press).

Boyson, R. (1981), 'The curse of the comprehensive', *Daily Mail* (London), 25 June 1981.

Bridges, D. (1976), 'The social organisation of the classroom and the philosophy of mixed ability teaching', *Cambridge Journal of Education*, vol. 6, nos 1/2, pp. 15–23.

Bridges, D. (1979), 'Why curriculum planning should not be "left to the experts"', *Journal of Philosophy of Education*, vol. 13, pp. 159–64.

Cambridge Journal of Education (1976), vol. 6, nos 1/2.

Caulfield, M. (1977), 'Mixed ability grouping at Bishop Douglass school', in *Mixed Ability Teaching in the Secondary School*, ed. B. Davies and R. G. Cave (London: Ward Lock), pp. 69–79.

Corbishley, P. (1977), 'Research findings on teaching groups in secondary schools', in *Mixed Ability Teaching in the Secondary School*, ed. B. Davies and R. G. Cave (London: Ward Lock), pp. 1–17.

Crosland, C. A. R. (1962), *The Conservative Enemy* (London: Cape).

Crosland, C. A. R. (1974), 'Comprehensive education', in *Socialism Now and Other Essays* (London: Cape), pp. 193–210.

Daunt, P. E. (1975), *Comprehensive Values* (London: Heinemann).

Davies, B. (1977), 'Meanings and motives in "going mixed ability"', in *Mixed Ability Teaching in the Secondary School*, ed. B. Davies and R. G. Cave (London: Ward Lock), pp. 18–40.

Deale, R. N. (1977), 'Assessment in the mixed ability group', in *Mixed Ability Teaching in the Secondary School*, ed. B. Davies and R. G. Cave (London: Ward Lock), pp. 80–98.

Department of Education and Science (1977), *A New Partnership for our Schools* (London: HMSO).

Department of Education and Science (1978), *Mixed Ability Work in Comprehensive Schools*, HMI series Matters for Discussion, No. 6 (London: HMSO).

Dooley, P., Smith, A., and Kerry, T. (1977), *Teaching Mixed Ability Classes* (Nottingham: University School of Education).

Elliott, J. (1976), 'The problems and dilemmas of mixed ability teaching and the issue of teacher accountability', *Cambridge Journal of Education*, vol. 6, nos 1/2, pp. 3–14.

Elliott, J. (ed.) (1978), *Hypotheses about Mixed Ability Teaching* (Cambridge: Cambridge Institute of Education).

Esposito, D. (1973), 'Homogeneous and heterogeneous ability groupings: principle findings and implications for evaluating and designing more effective educational environments', *Review of Educational Research*, vol. 43, pp. 163–79.

Ford, J. (1969), *Social Class and the Comprehensive School* (London: Routledge & Kegan Paul).

Fromm, E. (1956), *The Sane Society* (London: Routledge & Kegan Paul).

Gewirth, A. (1978), *Reason and Morality* (Chicago: Chicago University Press).

Gough, B., and McGhee, J. (1977), 'Planning for mixed ability', in *Mixed Ability Teaching in the Secondary School*, ed. B. Davies and R. G. Cave (London: Ward Lock), pp. 41–54.

Hargreaves, D. (1967), *Social Relations in a Secondary School* (London: Routledge & Kegan Paul).

Holt, M. (1976), 'Non-streaming and the common curriculum', *Forum*, vol. 18, no. 2, pp. 55–7.

Hoyles, E. M. (1975), 'Vauxhall Manor school', in *Case Studies in Mixed Ability Teaching*, ed. A. V. Kelly (London: Harper & Row), pp. 49–63.

ILEA Inspectorate (1976), *Mixed Ability Grouping* (London: ILEA).

Jackson, B. (1964), *Streaming: An Education System in Miniature* (London: Routledge & Kegan Paul).

Kelly, A. V. (1975), *Case Studies in Mixed Ability Teaching* (London: Harper & Row).

Kelly, A. V. (1978), *Mixed Ability Teaching: Theory and Practice* (London: Harper & Row).

Madgwich, S. (1980), 'Mathematics', in *Mixed Ability Teaching*, ed. C. Sewell (Nafferton: Nafferton Books), pp. 169–98.

Monks, T. G. (1968), *Comprehensive Education in England and Wales* (Slough: NFER).

Morrison, C. M. (1976), *Ability Grouping and Mixed Ability Grouping in Secondary Schools* (Edinburgh: Scottish Council for Educational Research).

Newbold, D. (1977), *Ability Grouping – the Banbury Enquiry* (Slough: NFER).

Nozick, R. (1974), *Anarchy, State and Utopia* (New York: Basic Books).

Peters, R. S. (1966), *Ethics and Education* (London: Allen & Unwin).

Plamenatz, J. (1975), *Karl Marx's Philosophy of Man* (Oxford: Clarendon Press).

Postlethwaite, K., and Denton, C. (1978), *Streams for the Future* (Banbury: Pubansco).

Rawls, J. (1972), *A Theory of Justice* (Oxford: Clarendon Press).

Reid, M., Clunies-Ross, L., Goocher, B., and Vile, C. (1981), *Mixed Ability Teaching: Problems and Possibilities* (Windsor: NFER/Nelson).

Sallis, J. (1977), *School Managers and Governors: Taylor and After* (London: Ward Lock).

Sewell, C. (ed.) (1980), *Mixed Ability Teaching* (Nafferton: Nafferton Books).

Williams, B. (1969), 'The idea of equality', in *Philosophy, Politics and Society: Second Series*, ed. P. Laslett and W. G. Runciman (Oxford: Blackwell), pp. 110–31.

Index